BLENDER 4.4
GUIDEBOOK

UNLOCKING THE POWER OF 3D
ANIMATION AND MODELING

BEN TAYLOR

TABLE OF CONTENTS

CHAPTER ONE

INTRODUCTION TO BLENDER 4.4

What's New in Blender 4.4

The discharge of Blender 4.4 brings various inventive highlights which bring way better usefulness together with speedier execution to improve imaginative yield. These are the foremost basic improvements in Blender 4.4:

1. **Enhanced User Interface**
   - **New Default Theme**: The modern default subject gives improved differentiate companioned by superior visual clarity in Blender 4.4 to support longer ceaseless work sessions.
   - **Improved Layout Customization**: The client interface permits board measuring at the side workspace alteration so clients can make personalized workflows.

2. **Performance and Speed Upgrades**
   - **Faster Rendering**: The Cycles rendering motor performs quicker since designers optimized it particularly for complex scenes to decrease in general rendering times.

Faster Rendering

o **Viewport Improvements**: Eevee motor presently offers progressed real-time shadows as well as reflections and presents by and large superior viewport productivity.

3. **Geometry Nodes Enhancements**

o **New Nodes**: The unused procedural modeling tool compartment incorporates numerous hubs that give progressed capabilities for geometry collection administration with made strides organize visualization.

o **Improved Usability**: The Geometry Hubs interface appears way better proficiency through moved forward plan which empowers higher-level procedural plan capabilities and devices.

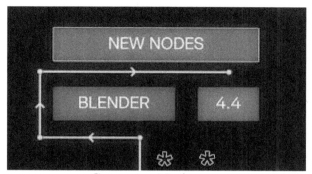
Geometry Nodes

4. Sculpting Improvements

- ○ **Dynamic Topology Updates**: The framework of Energetic Topology Overhauls gotten upgrades through execution and adaptability boost by actualizing speedier energetic topology overhauls.

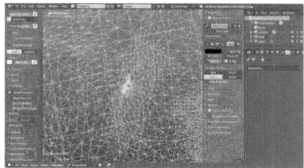
Dynamic Topology Updates

o **New Brushes and Masking Tools**: Blender 4.4 includes modern chiseling brushes along with progressed veiling instruments which disentangle advanced sculpting work.

5. **Grease Pencil Enhancements**

   o **New Brush Options**: Blender 4.4 expands its brush collection with progressed strokes and drawing highlights particularly planned for Oil Pencil clients which makes a difference make way better energized drawings.

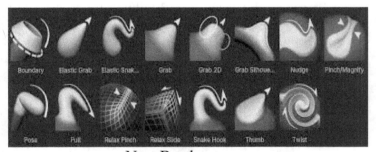

New Brushes

   o **Better 3D Tools**: Clients presently have made strides usefulness for making 3D Oil Pencil objects that disentangle the move between 2D and 3D working methods.

6. **Animation and Rigging Improvements**
   o **F-Curve Editing**: The chart editor gotten improvements to its complex activity bend dealing with highlights which included superior keyframe adjustment capabilities.
   o **New Rigging Tools**: Blender 4.4 brings less difficult programmed fixing highlights to the stage in expansion to improved apparatuses which let clients control armature misshapening in this way progressing character fixing methods.

7. **Asset Browser and Libraries**
   o **Improved Asset Management**: The Asset Browser received enhancements which improve the way users handle and browse materials together with models and brushes.
   o **Drag-and-Drop Functionality**: Users gain the capability to conveniently pull assets into scenes by dragging them from the Asset Browser to their destination.

8. **Simulations and Physics Updates**
   o **Fluid Simulation Enhancements**: The interface options delivered faster fluid simulations and enhanced stability leading

to better control during fluid simulation processes.

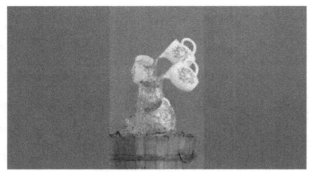
Fluid Simulation

o **Cloth and Soft Body Simulation Improvements**: Improved solvers in cloth and soft body simulation produce more natural outcomes at reduced computation duration.

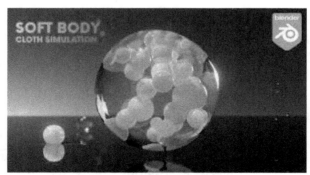
Soft Body Cloth Simulation

9. **Python Scripting and API Updates**
   - **Better Python Integration**: The Python API gets better due to recent updates which offer more capabilities for programmatic management of scenes and rigs and assets.
   - **New Add-ons**: New community add-ons now receive official support in Blender's add-on repository which extends the application's functionality even more.

New Add-ons

10. **Eevee and Ray Tracing**
   - **Ray Tracing Support**: Real-time ray tracing through Eevee received enhancements which improve its ability to produce genuine lighting effects as well as reflective and shadow effects.

11

o **Better Post-Processing**: The software now delivers enhanced post-processing effects that execute faster rendering of motion blur together with depth of field and bloom capabilities.

The latest Blender version 4.4 expands the possibilities of 3D modeling and animation together with simulation by offering advanced tools which empower both professional and casual users for superior creative results.

Interface Overview

Blender 4.4 provides an upgraded interface that simplifies user workflow while it provides accessible navigation and enhances overall usability in the software. The Blender interface consists of these main components as shown below:

1. The Layout

Blender features different main workspace areas in its default interface to deliver effective operational environment:

- **Top Bar**: The top bar offers necessary features for rendering and workspace and file system

12

management alongside workspace control functions.

- **Toolbar (Left Sidebar)**: Users can find selection tools and transform tools along with object creation options located on the left sidebar in the program interface.

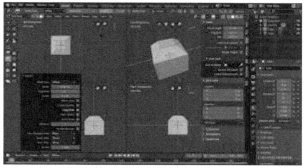

Toolbar (Left Sidebar)

- **Properties Panel (Right Sidebar)**: Properties Panel in the right sidebar contains settings for selected objects as well as material properties and modifiers and rendering elements. Every context (Object Material Scene and others) presents its specific controls within this area.
- **3D Viewport**: Through the 3D Viewport users experience their 3D scene directly because this region serves as their main interface point. Through

this workspace users can create models by animation and real-time visualization of objects.

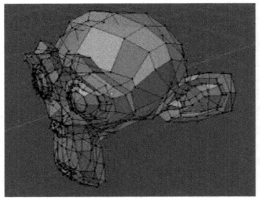
3D Viewport

- **Timeline**: The Timeline panel appears at the bottom part which enables users to control animation playback and keyframing for precise animation control.

Timeline

- **Outliner**: At the top-right corner of your screen the Outliner appears to display a structured view of your scene elements including objects lighting

14

cameras and other components which enables easy access to selection and control activities.

2. Workspaces

The modeling workspace lies among other pre-set workspaces in Blender 4.4 alongside departments for shading, sculpting and modeling and animation. The workspaces include specific design layouts and functions which accelerate your work process.

- **Modeling Workspace**: The default display for generating three-dimensional models appears in Modeling Workspace.

Modeling Workspace

- **Sculpting Workspace**: The sculpting workspace provides all required digital sculpting elements arranged in an optimal layout.
- **Shading Workspace**: The Shading Workspace directs its focus on material and texture development together with access to the Shader Editor feature.

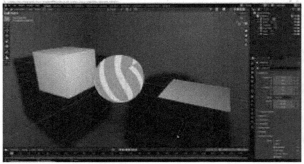
Shading Workspace

- **Animation Workspace**: Provides access to keyframe tools, the graph editor, and timeline.

Workspaces made by users can be developed to fulfill specific needs.

16

3. Menus and Contexts

The menus of Blender present their options through a sensibly arranged contextual framework. The application shows different main menu choices above based on which tool or mode you currently use.

- **Object Mode**: The Object Mode enables the handling of scene objects through moving and rotating and scaling actions.

Object Mode

- **Sculpt Mode**: The Sculpt Mode contains sculpting instruments and tools which work with formative topology mechanisms.
- **Edit Mode**: The mode for editing mesh geometry allows users to apply modifications such as adding vertices alongside edges and faces.

17

Edit Mode

- **Pose Mode**: The Pose Mode becomes active when users work on rigged characters and poses.

The right-click menu appears with commands based on where your current position is in the Blender interface.

4. Navigating the 3D Viewport

The 3D Viewport delivers most user interaction through its set of navigation tools that include:

- **Orbiting**: You can achieve orbital rotation through the scene when you press and hold the middle mouse button (MMB).

- **Panning**: The view movement through vertical and horizontal directions happens when you use Shift + MMB.

- **Zooming**: You have two choices to navigate using the mouse wheel for zooming: standard scroll or controlling the zoom motion with Ctrl + MMB.

- **View Aligning**: View Aligning functions are easily accessible through the numpad keys which enable users to access front, side, top, and camera views.

Selecting between solid, wireframe, and rendered views for different viewport shading modes becomes possible through adjustments of the viewport settings.

5. The Status Bar

The lowest part of the interface contains important information regarding the current frame number along with active tool definitions and memory utilization metrics. The interface shows helpful notification pop ups informing viewers about the active scene occurrences.

6. Tool Shelf (T Panel)

Users can enable access to their currently active tools and brush controls through the Tool Shelf system which becomes available by pressing the T key. This section adapts its shown content to match your current activity either in modeling or sculpting or painting.

7. Property Search and Quick Access

The search capability in Blender 4.4 provides a powerful tool which enables users to execute any functionality or setting through a combination of F3 button access or by pressing the spacebar. A complete understanding of tool names enables more advanced artists to boost their productivity through the search function.

8. Add-ons & Customization

Through its tall degree of modifiability Blender empowers clients to introduce add-ons which expand its capabilities through unused modeling highlights and resource stores. Clients can adjust the interface concurring to their needs through highlights that let them construct hotkeys and menus and characterize their claim workspaces.

9. Notifications & Tips

Blender 4.4 presents a advanced notice framework that produces time-based input around your activities and recognizable framework mistakes. Interior the program interface you may discover both accommodating tips and instructional exercises which give direction through your work prepare.

Conclusion

At to begin with look Blender may show up complex but its versatile interface makes a difference different working strategies through an organized framework. With customizable workspaces, instinctive route, and context-sensitive apparatuses, Blender 4.4 offers a effective environment for both beginners and advanced clients. You'll be able optimize your workflow by getting to be familiar with all highlights and format components of the interface.

Customizing Your Workspace in Blender 4.4

Through its broad customization highlights Blender gives clients with the capacity to adjust the interface components agreeing to their person workflow necessities. Proficient and amateur clients can improve their operation speed and work environment satisfaction by customizing their Blender workspace.

The taking after direct will appear you how to set up your Blender workspace inside Blender 4.4 agreeing to your person needs:

1. Understanding Workspaces in Blender

The Blender interface parts its substance into Workspaces that utilize predefined task-specific formats conveyed for modeling chiseling shading and movement capacities. Each workspace appears diverse board designs in expansion to task-specific editors along with tools that relate to that specific work.

The built-in workspaces in Blender are accessible by default but you'll be able make personalized formats without any issues.

2. Creating a Custom Workspace

To create your own workspace:

- **Step 1**: Navigate to the tab section at the top edge of the user interface which hosts workspace options such as Layout, Modeling, Sculpting and so on.

- **Step 2**: The workspace tabs' right-edge contains a plus icon (+) that novices can click during Step 2.

- **Step 3**: At the end of the workspace list a new tab will appear which can be named through right-clicking for the Rename option.

- **Step 4**: Begin customizing the workspace through panel adjustment and adding editors which you can place according to your needs.

Custom Workspace

3. Adding and Removing Panels

Blender's interface easily adapts because users can divide panels however they want and they can both align them together and adjust their dimensions to build custom environments.

- **Split Panels**: Use the crosshair cursor icon to split a panel during border navigation by left-clicking and dragging until satisfied with panel segmentation.
- **Join Panels**: Click and drag a panel border to unite it with another panel when you need them joined.
- **Resize Panels**: Panel resizing through drag actions is possible by touching panel edges. The editor panel sizes are completely adjustable through your manual control.

4. Configuring the 3D Viewport

You will spend most of your work time inside the 3D Viewport section. The 3D Viewport becomes more tailored to your needs when you adjust views alongside adding overlays while selecting appropriate settings through Blender interface:

- **Viewport Shading**: The top right corner of the 3D Viewport contains shading options such as Wireframe, Solid, Material Preview and Rendered which can be switched between. The tool allows users to create personal settings for particular work scenarios.

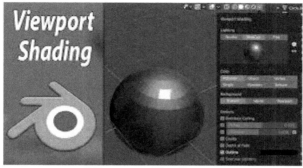

Viewport Shading

- **View Controls**: You can establish custom view presets through View Controls by using Ctrl + Alt + Numpad numbers (1, 3, 7) to develop front side and top perspective view then save them under View presets for swift modification.
- **Overlays and Gizmos**: The Overlays dropdown menu in the top right section allows users to turn different elements like grid and axis as well as annotations on and off. Gizmos provide easy access for navigation and transformation options which users can activate.

5. Customizing Toolbars and Panels

Blender provides toolbars and panels that alter their shown options based on the selected mode such as Object Mode or Sculpt Mode.

- **Tool Shelf (T Panel)**: You can enable the T Panel through the T key. You modify the tool selections through tool panel access by dragging different tools inside or outside. Tools in Blender can be rearranged into separate categories for related functionality.
- **Properties Panel (N Panel)**: The Properties Panel (N Panel) presents multiple option categories such as object details and materials together with modifiers. The interface sections can be expanded or collapsed to match your current work needs.

6. Custom Hotkeys and Keymap

Blender gives users the ability to modify their preferred hotkey combinations so they can improve their productivity.

- **Step 1**: Open the Preferences menu from Edit and select the Keymap option.
- **Step 2**: The search feature enables you to locate particular functions on Step 2 so that you can modify their assigned keys.
- **Step 3**: Users can create new keymap entries to assign multiple keys per command as well as restore factory default settings through Step 3.

You can optimize your workflow by assigning particular application components to individual hotkeys that you use frequently.

7. Adding Custom Add-ons to Your Workspace

Frontend users can use add-ons to extend Blender functionality by installing them from Preferences windows.

- **Step 1**: Start by navigating to Edit and clicking Preferences followed by Add-ons.
- **Step 2**: Users can perform searches for add-ons in this step and subsequently enable them with access to their settings.

- **Step 3**: Some additional features of your workspace will contain new panels with options you can utilize after activation.

When working with sculpting you should install an add-on that introduces new brushes or shortcuts to your workspace.

8. Saving and Loading Custom Workspaces

The customization work on your workspace merits to be spared within the future through these steps:

- **Step 1**: Your dynamic workspace plan will ended up spared in Blender records amid their spare prepare consequently.
- **Step 2**: Beneath the Inclinations menu tap Spare Inclinations to send out workspace settings with inclination inclinations for sparing over different ventures.

Custom workspaces can be stacked inside diverse files through this alternative to preserve reliable get to to your personalized setup amid modern venture work.

9. Using the Asset Browser for Quick Access

Blender 4.4 highlights an Resource Browser that enables users to oversee and recover materials at the side models surfaces and brushes and other resources inside the program. The workspace organizational highlights empower a slick working environment.

- **Drag-and-Drop**: Drag-and-Drop usefulness exists in Blender 4.4 to allow moment scene and workspace arrangement of resources straightforwardly from the Resource Browser for progressed effectiveness.

Drag-and-Drop

- **Custom Asset Categories**: You'll make particular categories inside the Resource Browser to disentangle your workspace resource administration.

10. Restoring Default Workspace Layout

You'll be able reset the Blender default workspace through a straightforward handle concurring to the taking after steps:

- **Step 1**: To start restoring the default workspace you wish to utilize the three level lines found at the best of the workspace tab on the screen.
- **Step 2**: The Reset to Default work quickly returns the workspace to the initial setup sketched out in Blender default parameters.

Conclusion

Blender 4.4 empowers clients to alter their workspace concurring to person necessities and work schedules. The accessible alternatives empower clients to work more effectively and comfortably by letting them adjust format settings and include boards and customize hotkeys and include add-ons. Investing time to make an ideal workspace in Blender will assist you utilize all of its capable highlights.

CHAPTER TWO

BASIC NAVIGATION & CONTROLS

Viewport Navigation in Blender 4.4

Effective management of the 3D Viewport stands essential for Blender work because it lets users connect with their scenes while boosting their productivity. The recent version of Blender 4.4 includes multiple functionality for smooth navigation throughout your three-dimensional workspace. Following is a guide that explains viewport navigation mastery:

1. Orbiting the Viewport

The orbiting function lets you rotate viewport views which enables you to view your 3D objects from different angles.

- **Method 1**: You can achieve viewport orbiting by using both methods: pressing middle mouse button (MMB) while keeping it click-activated and moving the cursor to rotate visual scope.
- **Method 2**: The Numpad keys (1, 3, 7) allow fast selection of viewport views such as Front and Right and Top. Pressing Ctrl + Numpad selects the opposite view (Back, Left and Bottom respectively).

Numpad keys with Ctrl activate the complementary view type (Back, Left, Bottom).

Note: The integration of this functionality requires you to select Edit → Preferences → Input → Emulate 3 Button Mouse on laptops that lack middle mouse buttons.

2. Panning the Viewport

When you enable panning it lets you slide your screen view in both directions and up and down without turning the perspective.

- **Method 1**: **Shift + Middle Mouse Button (Shift + MMB)** – Pressing Shift + MMB enables panning of the view by holding down Shift followed by maintaining Middle Mouse Button click until you finish the movement.
- **Method 2**: **Numpad 4, 6, 8, 2** – The Numpad provides two sets of commands for view panning which include 4 for left motion and 6 for right motion as well as 8 for upward movement and 2 for downward motion.

3. Zooming In and Out

You can manipulate image details through Zoom function which enables exact movement toward or from objects in the scene view.

- **Method 1**: **Scroll Wheel** – Zoom functions in Blender can be controlled by the mouse wheel whereby pushing upward enables closeup view and downward motion activates distant view.
- **Method 2**: **Ctrl + Middle Mouse Button (Ctrl + MMB)** – To zoom in or out with the third method you should first hold Ctrl and press the middle mouse button then move the mouse either up or down.
- **Method 3**: **Numpad + and -** – Incremental zooming can be accomplished using the Numpad + and - keys on the number pad.

4. Changing the View

Within Blender users can access standard views through multiple interface options which allows easier multi-perspective work with objects.

- **Front View**: **Numpad 1** – Switch to the front view of the scene.

- **Back View**: **Ctrl + Numpad 1** – Standard views change by using Ctrl + Numpad 1 key combination to view the scenes from the back side.

- **Top View**: **Numpad 7** – The switch to the top view of the scene can be achieved through pressing the Numpad 7 key.

- **Bottom View**: **Ctrl + Numpad 7** – Switch to the bottom view of the scene.

- **Right View**: **Numpad 3** – Switch to the right side view of the scene.

- **Left View**: **Ctrl + Numpad 3** – Switch to the left side view of the scene.

- **Camera View**: **Numpad 0** – Switch to the current camera view.

5. Perspective vs. Orthographic Views

Work in Blender requires the two viewing options of Perspective and Orthographic views.

- **Perspective View**: In Perspective View the scene presents realistic three-dimensional appearance where objects diminish in size according to their distance from the camera.

- o **Toggle Perspective/Orthographic**: Users can switch between perspective and orthographic view by pressing the Numpad 5 button.
- **Orthographic View**: This flat view mode shows objects without perspective distortion because it serves modelers in tasks needing precision such as alignment. Objects within orthographic view do not seem to get smaller even when positioned away from the camera.

6. Using the View Gizmo

A navigation functionality known as the View Gizmo resides within the upper right part of the 3D Viewport.

- Selecting one of the axis arrows found in the View Gizmo will change your viewport to that particular direction.
- Tapping on the cube button changes the interface to multiple default aspects (top, side, front and more).

- You can interactively orbit the view with the view sphere which operates as a 3D navigation widget. The view orientation can be adjusted more precisely through this particular tool.

7. Using the "Fly/Walk" Navigation Mode

In Blender 4.4 users gain access to the Fly/Walk Navigation Mode featuring controls that operate similarly to gaming controls with WASD.

- **Activate Fly Mode**: Press **Shift + ` (backtick)** (the key next to the number 1 key).
- **Move**: You can navigate forward using W key and left direction with A key and backward movement with S key together with right direction from D key.
- **Up/Down**: The keyboard shortcuts Q and E will allow you to move upwards and downwards.
- **Mouse Movement**: While Fly Mode is activated you can use the mouse to turn around the scene by moving it.
- **Exit Fly Mode**: Press the Esc key to leave the Fly Mode.

This mode serves well to speedily navigate big scenes and present a first-person view of your surroundings.

8. Frame Selected Object or Region

To enhance your scene work you should utilize the viewport framing capability that helps your selected regions or objects take up the full viewport space.

- **Frame Selected Object**: Press Numpad . (period) while having an object selected to zoom into and position the view directly on that object.
- **Frame Region**: A group of objects or selected portion of your scene can be framed using Numpad. after the desired selection.

Save time on scene refocusing by using this shortcut to center and zoom on recent creations or scene details.

9. Viewport Clipping

Viewport clipping offers designers a feature to determine what distances objects can become visible in camera views.

The reduction of performance strain remains possible due to this feature while working with large scenes.

- **Adjust Clip Start and End**: You must navigate to the View tab inside the Properties panel (press N to access it). The Clip section enables you to modify both Clip Start and Clip End values to specify which objects should be displayed at what distance in the viewport.

10. Viewport Navigation Tips and Tricks

- **Locking Views**: By pressing Ctrl + Alt + Numpad 0 you can lock an active view through an alignment process. Freezing views provides helpful control for composing particular camera shots.
- **Reset View**: The shortcuts Alt + Home lets you return to the default front view position.
- **Precision Navigation**: While holding down the Shift key you can perform precise movements when you are zooming or panning your interface.

Conclusion

The ability to navigate in Blender 4.4 viewport spaces efficiently enables proper modeling artwork as well as animation creation and presentation rendering in 3D environments. Blender provides intuitive scene exploration through different navigation options which include orbital movements followed by pan function and zoom capability and view transition capabilities. Your workflow speed and productivity will increase when you modify your navigation settings and learn each hotkey.

Essential Shortcuts in Blender 4.4

The latest Blender 4.4 version features extensive keyboard shortcut collection which helps users work faster. The essential Blender shortcuts for interface navigation and object management and key application utilizations appear below. The application has created these shortcuts to achieve better workflow efficiency and enhance user productivity in Blender.

1. Navigation Shortcuts

- **Orbit View**: The Middle Mouse Button (MMB) allows users to maintain a click for rotating the current view during Orbit View executions.

- **Pan View**: **Shift + MMB** – A combination of Shift and middle mouse button activates pan view function.

- **Zoom In/Out**: **Scroll Wheel** – The mouse wheel allows users to either expand or decrease the interface scale through simple wheel scrolling movements.

- **Zoom (Fine Adjustment)**: **Ctrl + MMB** – The middle button of the mouse combined with Ctrl triggers smooth zooming actions.

- **Frame Selected Object**: **Numpad . (period)** – User can center the selected object with Numpad. (period) while obtaining a zoomed view.

- **Front View**: Numpad 1

- **Back View**: Ctrl + Numpad 1

- **Top View**: Numpad 7

- **Bottom View**: Ctrl + Numpad 7

- **Right View**: Numpad 3

- **Left View**: Ctrl + Numpad 3

- **Camera View**: Numpad 0

2. Object and Scene Management

- **Select Object**: Users can perform object selection by right-clicking with their computer mouse as a default method or using left-click if mouse selection has been configured.

- **Select Multiple Objects**: Users can execute Multiple Object Selection either by using Shift + Right Click (default) or Shift + Left Click (if configured).

- **Deselect Object**: A achieves both object selection and deselection functions during object mode operation.

- **Grab/Move Object**: G

- **Rotate Object**: R

- **Scale Object**: S

- **Confirm Action (Move, Rotate, Scale)**: Enter

- **Cancel Action (Move, Rotate, Scale)**: To cancel any of these three operations, right-click the selection or hit Esc when using left-click selection.

- **Duplicate Object**: Shift + D

- **Delete Object**: X or Delete

- **Hide Object**: H

- **Unhide All Objects**: Alt + H

- **Toggle Object's Visibility**: Shift + H

- **Select All**: Twice pressing Key A will enable (or disable) All object selection.
- **Invert Selection**: Ctrl + I

3. Edit Mode (for Meshes)

- **Switch to Edit Mode**: Tab
- **Select Vertex/Edge/Face**: 1 (Vertex), 2 (Edge), 3 (Face)
- **Extrude**: E
- **Inset Faces**: I
- **Merge Vertices**: Alt + M
- **Loop Cut**: Ctrl + R
- **Knife Tool**: K
- **Fill Faces**: F
- **Select Edge Loop**: Alt + Right Click (Edge loop selection)
- **Select Face Loop**: Alt + Shift + Right Click (Face loop selection)
- **Subdivide**: **W** → Subdivide

4. Transforming Objects

- **Grab (Move) Object**: G
- **Rotate Object**: R
- **Scale Object**: S
- The operator key for X, Y and Z axes appears after users hit G, R or S.
- The combination of Shift + Tab enables snap functionality with Ctrl as a modifier for using snapping effects during movement of objects.
- Press Ctrl + A to execute Transformations of Location, Scale and Rotation.
- Use the period key to choose Pivot Point types including individual origin and median point.

5. Sculpting and Painting

- **Toggle Sculpt Mode**: To switch between modes press Ctrl + Tab while the top mode menu presents an alternative method.
- **Brush Size**: **F** – Use F to activate the command for adjusting brush dimensions.
- **Brush Strength**: You can modify brush strength through Shift + F key combination.

- **Symmetry Toggle**: The symmetry mode during sculpting can be enabled or disabled by using the key combination X.
- **Smooth Brush**: To activate smooth brush functionality users should click left mouse button after pressing the Shift key.
- **Undo/Redo**: Users can undo their actions by pressing Ctrl + Z while redo functions can be accessed through Ctrl + Shift + Z.

6. Animation Shortcuts

- **Insert Keyframe**: **I** – The shortcut I permits users to create a keyframe within the selected object or property.
- **Play/Pause Animation**: Spacebar
- **Go to Start Frame**: Shift + Left Arrow
- **Go to End Frame**: Shift + Right Arrow
- **Move to Next Keyframe**: Right Arrow
- **Move to Previous Keyframe**: Left Arrow
- **Toggle Auto Keyframe**: The timeline Record Button functions as Autonomate Tool Keyframes and users can also activate it by pressing Shift + Space.

- **Set Timeline Range**: User can establish timeline frame boundaries by using Shift + Left Click method.

7. Working with Materials and Shaders

- **Assign Material to Object**: Using Ctrl + 1-9 allows users to apply materials from existing material slots.
- **Go to Shader Editor**: Shift + F3 shortcut brings users to the material node editor through Shader Editor.
- **Open Material Properties**: Shift + F5
- **Preview Material in Viewport**: **Z** → Select Material Preview

8. Working with Modifiers

- **Add Modifier**: Users can activate the modifier selection through the use of Ctrl + 1-9 keyboard shortcut.
- **Apply Modifier**: To apply the currently highlighted modifier in the properties panel select Ctrl + A.

- **Toggle Modifier Visibility**: The shortcut Shift + Ctrl + M enables users to make all modifier visibility on and off simultaneously.

9. File and Scene Operations

- **New File**: Ctrl + N
- **Open File**: Ctrl + O
- **Save File**: Ctrl + S
- **Save As**: Ctrl + Shift + S
- **Export File**: Ctrl + Shift + E
- **Undo**: Ctrl + Z
- **Redo**: Ctrl + Shift + Z
- **Quit Blender**: Ctrl + Q

10. Viewport Overlays & Display

- **Toggle Wireframe View**: Z → Select Wireframe
- **Toggle Solid View**: Z → Select Solid
- **Toggle Rendered View**: Select the Rendered view in Z Mode by pressing the Z key.
- **Toggle Overlays**: Shift + Alt + Z

- **Show/Hide UI Panels**: N (for the right panel) and T (for the left toolbar)

11. Miscellaneous

- **Search Menu**: **F3** or **Spacebar** – F3 or Spacebar lets you find any selected tool setting or function by name in your system.
- **Toggle Full-Screen**: **Ctrl + Spacebar** – Maximize the current window or editor to full-screen.
- **Switch Editor Type**: **Shift + F10, Shift + F11, etc.** – Shift + F10 and Shift + F11 key combinations together with other Shift + F key combinations let you change views between Blender's Editor types.
- **View Port Shading**: **Z** – Toggles Between Solid Wireframe Material Preview and Rendered View Mode in the Screen.

Conclusion

Using Blender's keyboard shortcuts makes your work process run more effectively. By learning these main tools you will be able to shift through Blender's multiple features effectively. Testing these shortcuts repeatedly will make you work faster and better in Blender 4.4.

Selecting & Transforming Objects in Blender 4.4

Selecting and moving objects remains the base activity in Blender no matter what you do within the program including modeling, animation or scene setup. Blender 4.4 offers multiple tools and methods to control your selections of objects smoothly. This guide explains how to pick and move objects using Blender 4.4.

1. Selecting Objects

To use objects in Blender requires you to designate them as targets first. The application Blender offers multiple methods to pick either single items or groups of objects at once.

Basic Selection

- **Select Object**: You can activate selection with either a right-click action or by clicking if you changed the settings in Preferences.
- **Select Multiple Objects**: Press Shift to pick multiple objects one by one.
- **Select All Objects**: Press A once to select all elements and again to turn all selection off.

Select All Objects

- **Deselect Object**: Click outside the viewport to deselect an object (press the Alt key plus press the A key).

Advanced Selection Techniques

- **Circle Select**: To use circle selection click C on your keyboard. After enabling circle select mode you can draw a circle over any visible objects to include them in your selection.

- **Box Select**: Press B to switch to box select mode and draw a selection frame when you press and drag.
  - **Delete Selections in Circle Select**: Click Middle Mouse Button (MMB) to remove selected objects within the circle.
- **Lasso Select**: Left-click and hold Shift plus Control to make a freeform object selection.

Lasso Select

Selecting with the Outliner

- **Outliner**: You can choose objects immediately from the Outliner panel situated at the top right of the user interface. This function makes it simple to find and pick objects no matter how many items exist in the view or if they hide at a distance.

Select Linked Objects

- **Select All Linked by Material**: Click Ctrl + L and choose Materials to pick all items using the current material.
- **Select Linked**: Select Linked helps you choose all associated objects for the current selection through Ctrl + L and selecting from the available options.

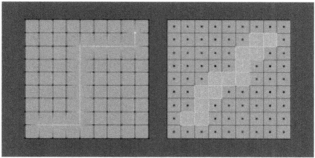

Select Linked

Select by Type

- **Select All Meshes**: When in Object Mode press Shift + G then Type → Mesh to highlight all mesh objects on screen.
- **Select by Group**: To pick by Group press Shift + G and then choose the Group selection mode.

2. Transforming Objects

After choosing objects you can adjust them by dragging them around or changing their orientation plus shape. These changes let you place objects in the right spot or modify their appearance.

Moving (Grab)

- **Move Object**: To pick and move selected items the G key brings up the move mode.
  - ○ **Constrain Movement to an Axis**: Press G then X, Y, or Z to move your selection in one plane using that specific axis (G+Z aligns movement on the Z plane).
  - ○ **Move Along View Plane**: Use Shift + Z to drag the object directly along its top and side planes.
  - ○ **Snap to Grid**: To align your object with the grid snap function hold Ctrl and move your mouse.

Rotating Objects

- **Rotate Object**: Hit R to turn the selected objects as you like.
  - ○ **Constrain Rotation to an Axis**: When you press R and then choose between X, Y, or Z

keys you can set the rotation restriction to the selected axis.

- ○ **Rotate in View Plane**: Use Shift + X as you rotate to control moves only within the Y-Z plane.

- ○ **Freeform Rotation**: Shift two times into R mode lets you make free rotating movements just like a moving Trackball controller.

Rotating Objects

Scaling Objects

- • **Scale Object**: Press S to change object dimension when objects are selected.

  - ○ **Constrain Scaling to an Axis**: Press S then X Y or Z to adjust object size specifically on chosen orientation.

- Uniform Scaling: After pressing S you can resize objects evenly in all directions by default.
- Scale in Two Axes: After pressing S and pressing Shift + X you will scale the object without moving it on the X-axis and Shift + Z brings that same result for the Z-axis.

Applying Transformations

- **Apply All Transformations**: After performing transformations on an object you can restore its movement position without changing its current scale or rotation. To do this:
  - **Apply Location**: Ctrl + A → Location
  - **Apply Rotation**: Ctrl + A → Rotation
  - **Apply Scale**: Ctrl + A → Scale
  - **Apply All**: Press Ctrl + A to Modify Position Rotation and Size Together.

Mirror Transformations

- **Mirror Transformation**: You can mirror object transformations through the Mirror Modifier or with Shift + Ctrl + M along an axis direction.

3. Using Gizmos for Transforming

Blender lets you work with transform gizmos which are viewport tools that help you transform objects with high accuracy.

- **Enable Gizmos**: Above the viewport you can turn on and off the Move, Rotate, and Scale Gizmos.
  - **Move Gizmo**: Using the Move Gizmo you can select and drag objects on the X, Y or Z axis with a button shape.
  - **Rotate Gizmo**: The circular gizmo rotates objects along three coordinate axes - X, Y, and Z.
  - **Scale Gizmo**: You can resize the object along specific axes when you drag the box-shaped gizmo.

Selecting gizmos from the top interface lets you switch between movement modes on the workspace or use Shift + Spacebar keypress to achieve the same effect.

4. Pivot Points

The pivot point lets you change where object transformations take place and Blender shows multiple options for selecting it.

- **Set Pivot Point**: You can open pivot point settings with a period key. The most common options are::
  - **Bounding Box Center**: Transforms apply to objects of the specified size from its center point position.
  - **Individual Origins**: Selecting elements at different points lets each one move from its unique starting position.
  - **3D Cursor**: You can set the 3D cursor point as your reference point for transforming objects across all 3 dimensions.
  - **Median Point**: Your chosen objects transform from the exact middle position between all of them.

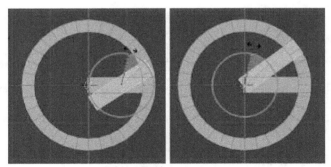

Pivot Points

5. Snapping Objects

Using Snapping helps you place objects at exact points with accuracy. The tool lets you attach objects to grid partitions or other objects at their endpoints.

- **Enable Snapping**: Selected Snapping turns on or off through Shift + Tab. The magnet icon inside your viewport header lets you switch snapping mode on and off.
- **Snap to Grid**: When you press Ctrl during movements of 3D object parts the system automatically locks to grid patterns.
- **Snap to Vertices/Edges/Faces**: To snap an object to nearest points select Ctrl while moving then the object will align to vertices edges or faces based on snapping preferences you set.

Snapping Settings: To control snapping settings:
- Select the desired snapping style under Snapping Options at the magnet icon spot.

6. Local and Global Transformations

You can modify your objects either by handling them locally or across all space in Blender.

- **Global Transformation**: By default the application transforms objects according to the world coordinate system.
- **Local Transformation**: You can transform objects accurately in their individual space using the N key to access properties and enabling Local Space under Transform settings.

7. Transform Orientation

During your transformation work you can select from different object orientations to work smarter in 3D space.

- **Global**: The basic coordinate axis matches the world orientation by default.
- **Local**: Aligned with the object's local axes.
- **Normal**: This mode links to movement based on each surface so objects stay oriented properly without rotation issues during creation.
- **Gimbal**: Aligns transformations to the current gimbal orientation.

Conclusion

Transformation and selection of objects plays an essential role in Blender 4.4 through which users create and arrange their three-dimensional spaces. The selection tools in

Blender include gizmos, precise scaling ability, rotating mechanics, and moving tools in addition to pivot point selection and snapping functionality and transformation orientation options. The mastery of these methods allows you to achieve greater work efficiency together with enhanced modeling precision that smooths your modeling and scene management process.

CHAPTER THREE

MODELING IN BLENDER 4.4

Mesh Editing Basics in Blender 4.4

The fundamental task of 3D modeling within Blender relies on mesh editing for all operations. Effective as well as efficient workflows for creating characters and environments and props depend entirely on mastering mesh editing fundamentals. The modeling tools in Blender version 4.4 are strong enough to precisely work with vertices edges and faces thus granting complete control of mesh elements. A total presentation to work altering in Blender adaptation 4.4 is given underneath.

1. Entering Edit Mode

A work requires Alter Mode status some time recently any alters gotten to be conceivable. Work altering starts after you actuate the Alter Mode since it empowers coordinate control of vertices edges and faces.

- **Switch to Edit Mode**: Users can switch between Object and Edit modes by pressing the Tab key while working in Blender 4.4.

- **Choose between Vertex, Edge or Face selection while working in Blender**:

- o **Vertex Selection**: Press 1 to select vertices.
- o **Edge Selection**: Press 2 to select edges.
- o **Face Selection**: Press 3 to select faces.

Edit Mode displays the object's geometric structure through wireframes that may turn into solid visualizations based on viewport shading choices.

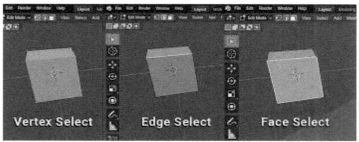

Entering Edit Mode

2. Selecting Components

After entering Edit Mode you must first select between vertices edges or faces for editing purposes. Blender provides multiple selection techniques for its components.

- **Select Vertex, Edge, or Face**: Right-click selection of a vertex or edge or face becomes possible through the "Select Vertex Edge or Face" series.

- **Multiple Selections**: You can use Shift with multiple mouse clicks to choose multiple vertices edges or faces in succession.
- **Select All**: To select all contents in your mesh just hit the A key once. A second press of the A key selects or deselects all currently selected mesh items.
- **Box Select**: The keyboard command B opens a selection box that allows you to choose components which you want to select.
- **Circle Select**: Users can activate circular selection by pressing the C key. Choose and pull your cursor to select object components that are found within the circle boundary. MMB can be used to disselect selected parts of your selection.
- **Lasso Select**: Users can activate the Lasso Select tool by pressing Ctrl + Shift + Left Mouse Button.
- **Select Linked**: When using Select Linked function you can pick a vertex edge or face afterwards activate Ctrl + L to detect adjacent mesh parts.

3. Manipulating Components

The selected components become available for transforming through movement and rotation as well as scaling. The primary operations of mesh modeling serve as its foundation for creating new designs.

Moving (Grab) Components

- **Move Components**: To move selected components you can activate the grab function by pressing G.
  - ○ **Constrain Movement to an Axis**: You may constrain axis-based movement by pressing X Y or Z right after activating G.
  - ○ **Snap to Grid**: The selected components will snap to the grid when you press and hold Ctrl while moving.

Rotating Components

- **Rotate Components**: Using keyboard command R allows users to rotate any selected component.
  - ○ **Constrain Rotation to an Axis**: Following R to initiate rotation you should press X, Y or Z to specify which axis rotation will occur along.

o **Freeform Rotation**: Freeform Rotation occurs when you consecutively press the R key twice (RR).

Scaling Components

- **Scale Components**: The command to scale components is available by pressing the S key.
    - o **Constrain Scaling to an Axis**: Press S to scale components after which selecting X, Y or Z will determine the axis of the scale operation.
    - o **Uniform Scaling**: Uniform Scaling will affect all selected components equally by default based on defaults.
    - o **Scale Along Two Axes**: Exclusion of Axis for Scale can be accomplished by simultaneously pressing Shift + Axis Key (such as Shift + Z) to preserve one axis while adjusting the other two.

4. Extrusion and Inset

The operations known as extrusion and inset are fundamental to mesh editing since they help users generate elaborate geometry.

- **Extrude**: Users can trigger extrusion of selected parts by pressing the E key. The selected components determine the origin of new geometry that results from extrusion.
  - ○ **Extrude Faces**: When using Face Selection mode to pick a mesh face staff can trigger new mesh face creation using the E key.
  - ○ **Extrude Along an Axis**: Selecting an axis for extrusion becomes possible after E press by using X, Y or Z keys.
- **Inset Faces**: Users can inset faces through the keyboard command I. After selecting the face you will create a dimensionally smaller duplicate version of it within its boundaries for purposes like building windows or doors or other recessed elements.

5. Loop Cuts and Edge Loops

The method of creating edge loops remains a standard procedure for enhancing model details. Inside Blender users can utilize a built-in function that allows quick insertion of edge loops.

- **Loop Cut**: The Loop Cut function becomes available by pressing Ctrl + R to add a loop cut. After pressing the shortcut:
  - ○ Hover over your mesh to preview the loop cut.
  - ○ Press the left click button to set the loop cut in its intended position.
  - ○ Mouse motion controls edge location before finishing with another mouse click.

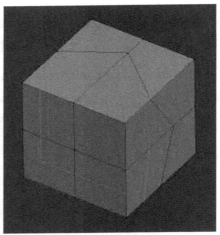

Loop Cuts

- **Edge Loop Selection**: Use Alt-key with right-clicking or left-clicking an edge to activate complete edge loop selection around the object.

Edge Loop

6. Merging and Splitting

Your mesh needs occasional modifications through part joining and part splitting.

- **Merge Vertices**: You can achieve Vertex Merge through the combination of Alt and M keys. Users have the option to merge selected vertices at the cursor or specific location or at the center position.
- **Split**: The Knife Tool (K) enables splitting edges or faces through drawn cuts to create fresh edges in your model.

7. Subdivision Surface Modifier

The Subdivision Surface Modifier delivers smooth mesh results through face subdivision procedures that work best for generating natural organic mesh structures with exceptional quality.

- **Add Subdivision Surface Modifier**: Click Object Mode before you go to the Modifiers tab where you should add Subdivision Surface Modifier.
- **Apply Subdivision Modifier**: After installing the proper modifier settings users should use the Apply button to execute the modifier application.
- **Subdivision Levels**: You can enhance geometric smoothness using more subdivision levels yet reduce specifics for speed by lowering the level count.

8. Proportional Editing

Using proportional editing lets you modify vertices, edges or faces because the changes extend to surrounding elements which results in more natural shapes.

- **Activate Proportional Editing**: Using Keyboard Shortcut Press you can activate or deactivate proportional editing.

- **Adjust Influence**: When applying movements or rotations or scaling components to objects the mouse wheel allows users to set transformation amounts on bordering geometry.

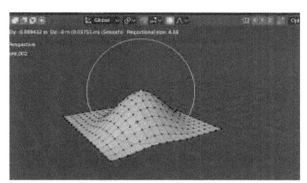

Proportional Editing

9. Transform Orientations and Snapping

Transform orientations supplement snapping tools to aid precise manipulation of your designs.

- **Transform Orientation**: You can modify the transformation orientation by pressing (period key). Some common orientations include:
  - **Global**: World space axes.
  - **Local**: The object's local space axes.

○ **Normal**: Aligned to the face normal of a selected face or edge.

Transform Orientation

- **Snapping**: The viewport header includes a magnet icon that enables snapping while Shift + Tab serves as an alternative method for snapping activation.
  ○ Choose the snap element: Users must select the desired snap element from the list which contains Increment, Vertex, Edge, Face, etc.
  ○ **Snap to Grid**: The transformation of components to grid positions becomes possible when you hold Ctrl key during the process.

10. Using the Knife Tool

Geometry mesh editing via precise cuts operates through the Knife Tool which can be accessed by pressing K.

- **Activate the Knife Tool**: To activate the Knife Tool press K and start clicking for cutting operations.
- **Make a Cut**: To place new mesh edges during a cut operation users can left-click the desired positions in their mesh.
- **Cancel Cut**: You can end the cut process through right-click action.

Using the Knife Tool

11. Symmetry and Mirroring

Through the useclusion of symmetrical tools you maintain one side of an object and the mirror tools update the opposite side automatically.

- **Enable Mirror Modifier**: You can enable Mirror Modifier by adding it to the Modifiers section to achieve mesh redirection along any chosen axis (X, Y, or Z).

- **Symmetry in Sculpting**: A sculptor can activate X-axis symmetry in their work to automatically duplicate their changes from one mesh side to the other.

Conclusion

The effective 3D modeling requires developers to learn fundamental mesh editing techniques inside Blender 4.4. Building complex shapes and structures remains possible through your capability to execute selections, movements, rotations, scaling, extruding and geometry cutting operations. Your control of modeling projects increases through the application of knife tool and loop cuts together with proportional editing and modifiers to your workflow. Regular practice of your basic mesh-editing skills via Blender 4.4 will lead you to produce advanced 3D models within a short period.

Modifiers (New & Updated) in Blender 4.4

Modifiers in Blender serve as a flexible tool which enables interactive and non-permanent adjustments to model shapes in three dimensions. The system helps users automate difficult processes and optimizes workflow activities then displays instant mesh modifications without permanently affecting its original structure. The modifications added in Blender 4.4 bring new modifiers together with recent updates of existing ones which enhance functionality alongside usability improvements. This article provides an overview of all the critical new modifiers available in Blender version 4.4.

1. Subdivision Surface Modifier (Updated)

The latest release of Blender 4.4 included important enhancements to its Subdivision Surface modifier. The Subdivision Surface modifier divides mesh surfaces and improves their geometric smoothness. The modifier appears in multiple projects to produce flowing organic forms.

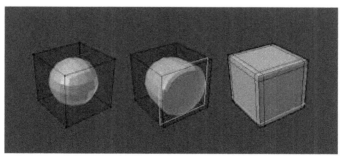

Subdivision Surface Modifier

- **New Features in Blender 4.4**:
  - ○ **Crease/Sharpness Control**: Edge and corner sharpness can be controlled more easily through the modifier interface in Blender 4.4.
  - ○ **Adaptive Subdivision**: The adaptive subdivision feature received better control in Blender 4.4 by allowing users to use geometric curvature patterns to decide where and how subdivisions will execute.
- **Usage**: Users can achieve mesh smoothing through the addition of the Subdivision Surface Modifier from the modifier tab. They should adjust subdivision levels accordingly. Edge Crease enables you to maintain sharp edges when performing subdivision.

2. Mirror Modifier (Updated)

In Blender environment the Mirror Modifier represents a fundamental pattern for achieving symmetry during the modeling process of characters together with vehicles.

- **New Features in Blender 4.4**:
  - **Mirroring on Multiple Axes**: The new release enables users to perform mirror operations simultaneously on X Y and Z axis alignment. The addition is beneficial for developing multiple symmetrical designs.
  - **Automatic Clipping**: The Clipping feature operates with multiple mirrored axes to enhance vertex alignment control when you work on the mirror plane.
  - **Extended Axis Options**: You gain better control of complex models through the ability to mirror across both custom or local axes with this option.
- **Usage**: The first step is to apply the Mirror Modifier then select the mirrored axis through the interface. Users can enhance their results through modification of the additional settings which include Clipping, Merge and Center.

3. Boolean Modifier (Updated)

The Boolean Modifier conducts mesh operations which include union functionality and also allows users to perform difference and intersection operations. This tool enables users to generate elaborate forms through mesh combination and subtraction operations.

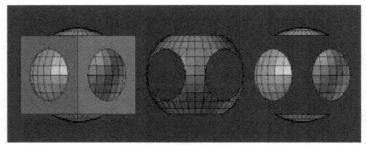

Boolean Modifier

- **New Features in Blender 4.4**:
    o **Better Performance**: The Boolean modifier runs faster and achieves more dependable results which lowers occurrence of artifacts while using complex boolean operations.
    o **Improved UI**: The user interface now shows better feedback through visual elements that enhance previews of Difference, Union and Intersect operations.
    o **Support for Multiple Inputs**: Multiple meshes can now be processed through the Boolean modifier because it supports more than two input meshes during operations.

- **Usage**: The Boolean Modifier can be utilized through its Usage section where users should choose between Union, Difference and Intersection operations. You should first choose which object needs modification and then activate the modifier.

4. Skin Modifier (Updated)

The Skin Modifier enables swift creation of organic surfaces across skeletal structures because most users utilize it to build initial meshes for character models and similar organic shapes.

Skin Modifier

- **New Features in Blender 4.4**:
    - **More Control Over Edge Flow**: The modifier allows users to exert greater

command when controlling mesh flow so they can direct how geometry elements arrange themselves near and around bones.

- o **Improved Visual Feedback**: Users benefit from improved visual feedback since skinner features better visual mapping of skin edges and vertices.
- o **Better Integration with Armature**: The integration of armature-based animation and rigging has been improved through the modifier so users need fewer manual interventions.

- **Usage**: Users can apply the Skin Modifier to a mesh while using Ctrl + A to assign bones to this object. When added to a mesh it will conform to the form of the bones automatically.

5. Wireframe Modifier (Updated)

With the Wireframe Modifier users can generate a wireframe outline around the geometrical layout of their models to produce stylized visual effects and artistic designs.

Wireframe Modifier

- **New Features in Blender 4.4**:
    - ○ **Thickness Control**: The wireframe thickness control has received improvements through more precise edge width management.
    - ○ **Solidify Mode**: The modifier features Solidify Mode that enables hollowed mesh generation through thickness controls suitable for building walls or frames.
    - ○ **Better Edge Preservation**: One of the improvements includes better maintenance of sharp edges and points during wireframe applications.
- **Usage**: Use the Wireframe Modifier on a mesh object while refining its Thickness value and additional settings for producing targeted results.

6. Displace Modifier (Updated)

Similar to the displacement modifier is the Displace modifier which uses textures or images and deforms mesh objects in three-dimensional space to create landscape features and watery effects. New Features in Blender 4.4:

Displace Modifier

- **New Features in Blender 4.4**:
    - **Texture-Based Displacement**: Blend 4.4 allows you to select textures such as Noise and Voronoi among others for geometric displacement functions.
    - **Improved Texture Sampling**: An improved mode traces textures to produce superior mesh displacements.
    - **Support for Multiple Axes**: Users can simultaneously displace their meshes within X, Y and Z axis boundaries to gain better

control when working with complex displacement operations.

- **Usage**: Users need to implement the Displace Modifier while adding a texture for their work. Select the displacement axis and modify its amount using the Strength parameter.

7. Decimate Modifier (Updated)

For real-time applications and game engine performance optimization you should use the Decimate Modifier because it reduces mesh polycount effectively.

Decimate Modifier

- **New Features in Blender 4.4**:
  - **Improved Triangulation Algorithm**: New implementation of Triangulation Algorithm

through updated decimation process produces more organized results that minimize artifact formation.

- o **Planar and Angle-Based Reduction**: Planar and Angle-Based Reduction has been added to the modifier which enables users to have more precise decimation control.
- o **Preserve Shape**: The Shape Preserving feature of the updated modifier maintains mesh structures with improved algorithms which are perfect for polycount optimization while keeping detailed features intact.
- **Usage**: Three possible methods through the Decimate Modifier help users reduce polygon counts: adjust the Ratio value or activate Collapse, Un-Subdivide or Planar functions.

8. Geometry Nodes Modifier (New)

The main update to Geometry Nodes in Blender 4.4 made this tool essential for working with procedural methodologies. The tool serves as an effective solution for making both procedural forms and animated structures.

- **New Features in Blender 4.4**:
  - **Enhanced Node System**: The procedural geometry creation capabilities for the node system received better performance improvements through enhanced system functionality with new nodes in version 4.4.
  - **Real-Time Feedback**: The procedural modification workflow received improvement through Geometry Nodes real-time feedback which gives immediate visual feedback to users.
  - **More Built-In Nodes**: Blender 4.4 includes additional built-in nodes to facilitate procedures related to object randomization together with instance capabilities and geometry editing tasks.
- **Usage**: Starting procedural node networks requires the addition of the Geometry Nodes Modifier followed by the opening of the Node Editor window. With nodes you can create the outline for your object which depends on multiple inputs along with adjustable parameters.

9. Simplify Modifier (Updated)

The Simplify Modifier helps users decrease mesh complexity which enables optimization and low-poly previews of complex 3D models.

Simplify Modifier

- **New Features in Blender 4.4**:
  - **Automatic Level of Detail**: Objects within Blender automatically receive detail adjustments depending on how far the camera stands from them.
  - **Optimized for Performance**: The simplification algorithms of this modifier received optimization to achieve better performance results with decreased visual degradation.

- **Usage**: Users can apply the Simplify Modifier followed by adjustments of its control settings to control both detail levels and simplified quality.

Conclusion

The modeling and optimization process using Blender 4.4 receives enhanced efficiency through new and updated modifiers that provide you with greater flexibility during 3D asset creation and texturization. Blender 4.4 expands your artistic toolbox through improved modifications of existing features such as Subdivision Surface, Mirror and Boolean and via the introduction of the Geometry Nodes Modifier combined with enhanced performance of Decimate and Simplify tools. Learning to control these modifiers leads to complete utilization of all Blender tools.

Sculpting & Retopology in Blender 4.4

Shaping through modeling and planning the surface topology remains vital for digital artists working with natural forms as well as intricate models of living beings and their habitats. Blender 4.4 includes important enhancements to its sculpting tools and it now offers integrated retopology capabilities which enhance performance for all users. The following section presents complete instructions about Blender 4.4's fundamental sculpting and retopology tools together with their new capabilities.

1. Sculpting Overview

The sculpting process enables users to build and finalize three-dimensional objects naturally through their fingertips. Through Sculpt Mode of Blender users can access multiple brushes which allow them to reshape their model through pushing, pulling, smoothing and refining operations on its geometry.

Entering Sculpt Mode

- Start the sculpting process by selecting an object then use Tab to enter Sculpt Mode or chose the mode from the interaction options found in the viewport top-left corner.
- In the left panel under the Tool Shelf (T) stands the collection of sculpting tools along with their settings such as brushes and symmetry options and strength controls.

2. Sculpting Brushes & Tools

Users now have access to new drawing tools and the Blender 4.4 software raises the capabilities of its current tools. Important brushes and tools available in Blender include the following components:

- **Draw Brush**: The Draw Brush functions as a tool that helps users both push and add geometry to generate more volume for their model.
- **Clay Brush**: A powerful brush tool called Clay Brush exists to rapidly add material while replicating clay effects.
- **Smooth Brush**: The smooth brush combines with other details to create a smooth area in models.
- **Grab Brush**: The Grab Brush provides a simple method to easily transfer large quantities of geometry.
- **Inflate Brush**: Through the Inflate Brush you can expand the mesh sections outward.
- **Crease Brush**: The Crease Brush allows users to generate sharp creases or folds which are essential when detailing wrinkles or seams in their models.
- **Trim and Flatten Brushes**: The Trim and Flatten brushes allow users to smooth mesh surfaces while allowing them to remove extraneous details.

New Brushes in Blender 4.4

- **Simplify Brush**: The Simplify Brush makes surfaces less complex to work with when you sculpt because it enables fast basic shape definition.

- **Smooth Depth Brush**: The Smooth Depth Brush enables detailed mesh smoothing by allowing artists to separate the contour process from specific details when using high-poly meshes.

3. Sculpting with Multiresolution Modifier

Sculpting needs the Multiresolution Modifier because it provides essential capabilities for precise sculpting work. Through this tool you can break down your mesh at multiple stages thus obtaining great precision when modifying your model at various resolution points.

- **Preserve Shape**: The modifier maintains mesh shape so users can switch between multiple levels without sacrificing details that come from higher subdivision settings.

- **Sculpt at Different Levels**: Subdivision levels should be selected according to the type of sculpting work since broad strokes work best on lower levels but precise details require higher levels.

- **Enable Multiresolution Modifier**: The first step involves the addition of Multiresolution Modifier through the modifiers tab. You can divide the mesh into sections while choosing from various detail levels.

Multiresolution Modifier

4. Dyntopo (Dynamic Topology)

Dyntopo stands as a leading functionality within Blender 4.4 to insert dynamic geometry while sculpting because it works perfectly for detailed organic shapes.

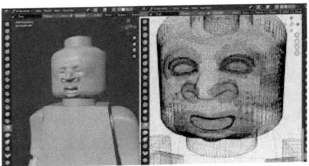

Dyntopo (Dynamic Topology)

- **Enabling Dyntopo**: Enable Dyntopo through the top bar control during Sculpt mode operations. The top bar provides an option enabling Dyntopo so users can refine mesh details during sculpting.

- **Resolution Settings**: You can define the resolution levels for dynamically subdivided meshes through resolution settings which let you create detailed zones.

- **Refine Areas**: With Detail Size users can determine the extent of added detail in selected model regions. The mesh geometry simplifies when you increase the value setting while reducing the value suits for better detail representation.

- **Auto Symmetry**: Auto Symmetry is a vital functionality that ensures equal distribution of your sculpting work across X, Y, or Z dimensional axes to perform better character and symmetrical object modeling workflows.

5. Sculpting with Layers

The introduction of Sculpt Layers in Blender 4.4 enabled users to work without destroying their original meshes through the addition of separate sculpted detail layers.

- **Create Layers**: Users can generate brand new sculpt layers from within the Sculpt Mode panel for proper storage of their changes. Model details are easily manage through various on/off and show/hide and delete functions triggered by this functionality.
- **Layer Brush**: The Layer Brush enables users to apply artistic elements to different layers which gives them the ability to modify or erase added details after painting.

6. Sculpting Tools Enhancements in Blender 4.4

Blender 4.4 improves sculpting tools through multiple performance improvements during the creative process:

- **Performance Boost**: performance has improved in Blender 4.4 for high polygon meshes because recent optimizations made the process less delayed and faster than before.

- **Brush Customization**: The Brush Settings tab in Blender 4.4 provides advanced options which let you modify brush shapes together with their texturing and behavioral characteristics.

- **Improved Symmetry Options**: Users can now control the brush effects on symmetrical model sections better thanks to improved symmetry options in the sculpt function.

7. Retopology Overview

Blender users create retopologies through the process of mesh creation using more efficient topology structures to replace high-polygon sculpted meshes. Blender 4.4 provides tools for retopology which users can access more easily while working with an intuitive interface.

8. Retopology Tools in Blender 4.4

The retopology process in Blender 4.4 gets simplified through various available tools for users.

Quad Remesh

- **New in Blender 4.4**: A major enhancement of the Quad Remesh tool marks its debut appearance in Blender version 4.4. The tool creates meshes with quads based on high-poly objects that improve both the predictability and ease of retopology.

- **Settings**: The topology patterns along with remesh density and smoothness settings in Blender 4.4 allow users to achieve well-structured meshes appropriate for animation work and additional sculpting.

Snapping to Surface

- **Surface Snapping**: The Surface Snapping feature of Retopology Mode enables users to place vertices directly to your model surface so they can build their new mesh over high-poly structures.

- **Snapping Options**: The controls for placing new elements include a selection between Vertex, Edge and Face snapping which dictates the model placement relationship.

Snapping to Surface

Poly Build Tool

- The Poly Build Tool enables users to draw vertices and edges manually so it serves as a valuable tool for focused retopology work in specific areas.

- **Quick Fill**: The Quick Fill feature allows quick polygon generation between vertices to produce efficient mesh cleaning.

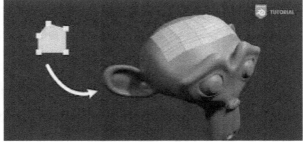
Poly Build Tool

Grease Pencil for Retopology

- The Retopology workflows now incorporate Grease Pencil more easily. The tool enables users to draw interactive references on their model for ultimate geometry creation assistance.

- **Guide Optimization**: Guide Optimization allows you to use Grease Pencil references while creating optimal edge loops and mesh flow during the retopologization process.

9. Retopology Workflow Tips

- **Start with a Base Mesh**: You should begin retopology by creating base geometry from either a basic form or a Quad Remesh until you add sufficient new mesh components.

- **Topological Flow**: Surface snapping should be used constantly to make sure your retopology mesh remains faithful to the sculpted model.

- **Use Surface Snapping**: Some parts of the mesh do not require excessive details which makes them suitable for simplification.

- **Simplify Areas**: Less significant regions should get simplified meshes in order to minimize the number of poly elements.

10. Retopology with Auto-Retopo Addon

The latest Blender 4.4 offers an Auto-Retopo addon that performs automatic tasks during the retopology operation. The retopology generator produces automatic quad-based topologies when you run a button command.

- **Use Auto-Retopo**: The Auto-Retopo option is located in the Object Mode menu for use. The Blender software evaluates the geometry to produce a professionally retopologized mesh.
- **Manual Adjustment**: Following retopology generation users can enhance areas needing more detail by employing Snapping together with Poly Build tools.

11. Sculpting to Retopology Workflow

The best way to execute efficient retopology and sculpting workflows requires both processes to function together smoothly:

1. **Start with Sculpting**: Begin Sculpting through Blocking Out Core Shapes by Using Sculpting Instruments that Include Dyntopo and Multi resolution.

2. **Retopologize**: After finishing sculpt work users should use Quad Remesh or Poly Build to generate a low-poly mesh structure with simple topology through retopology.

3. **Add Detail**: Low-poly artists have two options to transfer high-poly details post-retopology: they can sculpt new details or use normal maps, displacement maps and bump maps.

4. **Bake Details**: Baking tools located in Blender enable users to transfer high-poly details from the original model onto the low-poly mesh retopologization before using the object in real-time applications or animations.

Conclusion

Blender 4.4 delivers a creative environment through its sculpting and retopology tools that enables artists to produce outstanding 3D models with high quality. Donut brushes and related functionality and modifiers now allow artists to enhance their model details without difficulty while the redesigned retopology workflows along with automatic tools help simplify clean geometry generation. The ability to excel at sculpting and retopology in Blender 4.4 enables artists to produce professional-standard models that can be used for animation, gaming and 3D printing purposes.

CHAPTER FOUR

LIGHTING & RENDERING

Eevee vs. Cycles Updates in Blender 4.4

Both Eevee and Cycles of Blender 4.4 received essential enhancements that upgraded their rendering power while improving operational efficiency for different projects. The real-time Eevee engine establishes speed and interactivity as its core features yet Cycles stands as the ray-tracing engine which focuses on making physically precise high-quality images. The enhancement of both engines in Blender 4.4 becomes crucial for project choice because users need speed or photo-realistic results.

1. Eevee Updates in Blender 4.4

Eevee stands as Blender's real-time rendering engine because it provides speedy operations and finds applications in production settings that require instant render feedback. The latest Blender 4.4 release provides significant improvements that benefit users who work with Eevee animation along with live previews during interactive production sessions.

Eevee Updates

A. New Features in Eevee

- **Improved Lighting Models**: The lighting models in Eevee receive enhanced capabilities which produce more realistic outcomes particularly during light reflection and bleeding and surface reflection analysis. Enhancements in material-light interactions strengthen both the depth and realism of scenes.

- **Volumetrics Optimization**: The Eevee volumetric highlights (counting smoke and haze) display moved forward execution and quality characteristics. The exactness of volumetric rendering has expanded and it coordinating way better with lighting and shading impacts through HDRIs and light sources.

- **Screen Space Reflections (SSR) Improvements**: The developers have improved Screen Space

Reflections in Eevee which delivers enhanced reflection capabilities alongside better surface reflection fidelity. The software delivered better performance while processing reflective materials including glass and water.

(SSR) Screen Space Reflections

- **Motion Blur Enhancements**: Movement Obscure Improvements inside Eevee accomplish optimized execution for livelinesss of fast-moving objects and scenes. The modern addition strategy accomplishes smoother movement obscure moves all through the framework.

- **Better Depth of Field (DOF)**: The Profundity of Field impact in Blender form 4.4 gotten an imperative upgrade that conveys made strides authenticity nearby superior visual quality for the impact. Unused DOF impacts in Blender 4.4 convey improved common bokeh and focal point impacts that progress the visual offer of render ventures that utilize this highlight.

Depth of Field

B. Performance Enhancements

- **Faster Real-Time Previews**: Blender 4.4 upgraded the speed of Eevee rendering for complex scenes amid real-time sneak peaks. Real-time sneak peaks perform superior within the unused motor adaptation since its optimizations empower smooth sneak peaks of scenes that have complex effects and lighting beside expansive areas.

- **Improved GPU Utilization**: The made strides advanced GPU back in Blender 4.4 leads to prevalent equipment execution all through different frameworks. The way better utilization of GPU assets improves Eevee's real-time rendering when utilized for gaming resources generation nearby virtual generation and structural visualization ventures.

2. Cycles Updates in Blender 4.4

Cycles gives Blender clients with a ray-tracing innovation that makes exceedingly practical symbolism with exact exactness. Clients who require reasonable visual results for item exhibits and uncommon visual impacts work as well as building plan ought to utilize Cycles since it conveys prevalent photorealistic comes about but works at a slower rate than Eevee. The most up to date form of Blender 4.4 brings different improvements to Cycles that progress speed beside optimization and accuracy.

A. New Features in Cycles

- **Intel® Embree Integration**: Blender 4.4 includes Intel® Embree Integration as part of its new features which brings high-performance Embree ray-tracing kernel for efficient ray traversal to Cycles. The combination of Intel Embree integration produces faster rendering speeds during the process of rendering scenes with complicated geometry and complex light paths. Users who operate Intel CPUs will experience major speedups in how long their rendering tasks take to complete.

- **Denoising Improvements**: A significant update occurred with the Cycles denoising algorithms. The OptiX and NLM (Non-Local Means) denoising methods offer faster more efficient noise reduction through improved denoising techniques. The engine produces smooth outcomes and runs faster because of reduced samples needed for the process.

- **Adaptive Sampling Improvements**: The adaptive sampling feature in Cycles receives improved operational efficiency through recent optimizations. An improved rendering engine spends computational resources on parts of the scene that need more sampling data to expedite the overall rendering time and eliminate noise in detailed scenes.

- **Principled Volume Shader Updates**: The Principled Volume Shader received updates to improve its capabilities for developing volumetric materials including smoke fire and liquids. More advanced volume effects become attainable because of recent updates making the process simpler to execute successfully for both effects work and natural-looking scenes in visual art.

Principled Volume Shader

- **Hair Rendering Improvements**: Cycles deals with hair data more effectively to provide superior hair rendering capabilities including transparent and light-scattered effects.
- **Light Sampling and Path Guiding**: The new Cycles 4.4 implementation includes enhanced path guiding along with updated light sampling capabilities to optimize animations of glass

materials and effects from reflections and caustics of light paths. Such methodology results in enhanced rendering through decreased ray usage particularly in situations where various light interactions occur.

B. Performance Enhancements

- **Faster CPU Rendering**: The Cycles 4.4 update delivered both Intel Embree and additional CPU rendering speed optimizations which result in quicker performance throughout different hardware systems. Users of multi-core CPUs experience performance improvements because their system distributes resources more efficiently.

- **GPU Rendering Enhancements**: Cycles performs GPU-accelerated rendering superior much appreciated to its back for NVIDIA RTX GPUs beside AMD GPUs which upgrades speed over numerous equipment stages. The speed of GPU rendering has experienced considerable progression for computer clients who have high-end design cards.

- **Optimized CUDA/OptiX Backend**: The CUDA and OptiX backends which serve NVIDIA GPU clients have experienced performance-based advancements that boost beam following and upgrade in general speed. Clients can make faster and smoother renders since of how the framework handles complex activity's or scenes.

3. Eevee vs. Cycles: When to Use Each

Eevee and Cycles work as unmistakable rendering powers in spite of the fact that they give partitioned capacities to fulfill different venture requests. The taking after table illustrates how to choose between Eevee and Cycles based on particular needs:

Eevee vs Cycles

- **Eevee**:
    - Best for real-time sneak peaks, livelinesss, and intuitively work.
    - Clients who create gaming components and conduct virtual generation as well as make

movement design will achieve optimal results with this motor.

- o You ought to select Eevee after you require fast input through its speed in spite of the fact that its yield compromises true-to-life comes about (such as design walkthroughs or vivified figures).

- o The motor works best with scenes that dodge the require for totally reasonable representations however surpass straightforward drawing levels.

- **Cycles**:
  - o Best for photorealistic rendering, visual impacts, and item visualization.

  - o The framework exceeds expectations at challenging brightening setups beside troublesome substance creation (counting glass, water and metal things) and exact models.

  - o When precision along side quality matter over render time one ought to select this alternative (such as film generation and practical item creation and architectural visualization).

○ Still pictures and movement obscure, profundity of field impacts and exact light recreation at tall quality gotten to be conceivable utilizing this setting.

4. Conclusion

The upgrade in Blender 4.4 adds major enhancements to Eevee and Cycles which have enhanced their project application range. The performance enhancements of Eevee combined with its new functionality make it ideal for quick interactive operations along with Cycles' performance upgrades making it better suited for creating high-quality photorealistic results. One must select the engine according to project requirements- Eevee works best for projects which require rapid execution together with live interaction and Cycles remains the top choice if photorealistic effects and sophisticated lighting solutions are needed. Users in Blender 4.4 can select between fast rendering or precise results through the incorporation of Eevee and Cycles engine pair.

HDRI Lighting in Blender 4.4

Tall Energetic Extend Imaging (HDRI) gives 3D rendering devices with a solid arrangement for lighting procedures.

Your scenes advantage from reasonable and characteristic lighting through HDRIs since these pictures display brightness levels extending from dim shadows all the way to strongly highlights. The upgrade in Blender 4.4 provides improved performance for HDRI lighting which enables effortless implementation in both Eevee and Cycles render engines. The introduction of this section explains fundamental concepts about HDRI lighting benefits together with guidelines for Blender 4.4 project implementation.

1. What is HDRI Lighting?

The light source of HDRI lighting consists of high dynamic range images which create natural, environment-based illumination that responds correctly to your scene geometry. The high dynamic range information within HDRI images exceeds normal picture formats which make them suited for lighting simulation of actual environment interactions.

- **HDRI Images**: The creation of HDRI images originates from taking 360-degree panoramic photographs of actual surroundings or locations. A dynamic range in these images enables storage of lighting contrasts from deep shadows to light highlights.

- **Benefits of HDRI**: Using HDRIs for lighting can create more accurate reflections, realistic global illumination, and natural ambient light, which results in more convincing renders.

2. How HDRI Lighting Works in Blender

With Blender 4.4 HDRI lighting is a cinch to include by the World settings in the Shader Editor or in the Properties Panel. Here's how HDRI lighting works:

- **World Shader**: HDRIs are usually applied into the World shader in Blender. The word shader manages the environment lighting and background of your scene. Using an HDRI image in the world shader will do full light your scene, and so give reflection of your environment.
- **Environment Texture**: To apply an HDRI, you put it under the Environment Texture node in the Shader Editor and plug it into World's Background Shader. This will light and colored the background in the scene.
- **Reflection and Refraction**: Employing HDRI images for governing reflections that are realistic to

the environment. For instance, a HDRI of a bright sky will make realistic reflective effects on metals, glass and water.

3. Setting up HDRI Lighting in Blender 4.4

Here is a simple introduction of how to set up HDRI in Blender 4.4:

Step 1: Set the Render Engine to Cycles or Eevee

- One render engine selected open project in Blender. HDRI lighting is available to both Cycles and Eevee but keep in mine Cycles will be giving more accurate outcome especially for reflection and global illumination.

Step 2: Go to the World Properties Panel

- On the Properties Panel Select fist tab- The World (little globe icon).
- You will see a Default Background shader, which controls the environmental lighting.

Step 3: Add the HDRI Image

- Select the World node in the Shader Editor then add an Environment Texture node through the Shift + A menu.

- Press Open in the Environment Texture node and choose your HDRI file which normally ends with .hdr or .exr.

Step 4: Connect the HDRI to the World Shader

- Use the Environment Texture node to connect to the color input of the Background shader. This connects the HDRI texture to modify the lighting for the scene.

Step 5: Adjust HDRI Strength

- You can adjust the HDRI lighting effects by changing the Strength setting in the Background node controls. Increasing the Strength setting will make the HDRI environment brighter but decreasing it will weaken its lighting intensity.

Step 6: Set the Mapping (Optional)

- To modify the HDRI direction use a Texture Coordinate node with a Mapping node to scale and rotate the HDRI output.

4. Advanced HDRI Lighting Features in Blender 4.4

In Blender 4.4 users now have more ways to control and modify their HDRI lighting setups.

A. HDRI Rotation and Positioning

- **Mapping Node**: The Texturing and Mapping nodes help you set the right HDRI orientation when direct light sources in your scene require movement.

- **Spherical Mapping**: Spherical Mapping helps the HDRI light match the shape of your 3D scene through automatic wrapping.

B. HDRI Light Falloff and Directional Lighting

- **Light Falloff**: You can set up how HDRIs add light in your scene by setting the light falloff values. Use this tool to let the light fade into nothing or decrease its strength when your light source moves away from the setup. This option works best for outdoor lighting projects.

- **Directional HDRIs**: An HDRI from an outdoor setting will usually have direct sunlight when used as its lighting source. You adjust the HDRI rotation setting to select how sunlight shines on your scene.

C. HDRI Filtering in Eevee

- **Eevee Performance Optimizations**: In Blender 4.4 Eevee gained new technology that makes HDRI lighting run smoother. Creators now have filters that smooth out HDRI lighting effects and make reflections and shadows appear better in Eevee.

D. Multiple HDRI in a Scene

- Place different HDRIs over one another to build detailed lighting environments in Blender for special effects and gaming content.

5. Benefits of Using HDRI Lighting

- **Realistic Lighting**: HDRI lighting creates authentic natural lighting by representing how light acts in our world. This lighting technique reproduces how lighting mixes between objects and shows what the real world environment reflects.

Realistic Lighting

- **Global Illumination**: HDRIs can show accurate results for global illumination which means the indirect light that hit surfaces before bouncing back into your scene. The light appears more realistic in the scene because of this approach.

- **Ease of Use**: You can substitute difficult lighting setups with HDRIs since they are simple to handle. An HDRI brings lighting and background into your scene all at once which saves work on lighting setup.

- **Reflective Materials**: Using HDRIs gives you realistic reflections because they take their data from the environment picture stored in each HDRI.

6. Practical Uses for HDRI Lighting

- **Product Visualization**: By using HDRI lighting you can build studio environments that give products natural light display and show accurate shine and dark areas.

- **Architectural Rendering**: Audiovisual studios employ HDRIs to represent how daylight and nighttime lighting affects outdoor spaces in building plans.

- **VFX and Virtual Production**: Virtual Production uses HDRI lighting for ideal background illumination during 3D object integration into real scenes.

- **Game Asset Lighting**: Game developers use HDRIs to improve computer-generated asset lighting because they create lifelike environmental lighting.

7. Conclusion

The latest version of Blender 4.4 provides HDRI lighting functions for creating believable lighting effects in 3D scenes. No matter which tool you use Eevee or Cycles HDRIs give you an effective way to reproduce natural lighting and reflection results. HDRI lighting receives new and better capabilities within Blender 4.4 enabling you to work with it effortlessly in your projects.

Real-Time Rendering Tips in Blender 4.4

The latest Blender release enhanced Eevee real-time rendering technology making it more effective at its job. The instant display of your work through real-time rendering supports all your creative activities and saves you significant time in your projects. To create top-quality results at top speed you need to follow important rendering techniques. This area lists successful methods for real-time rendering in Blender 4.4.

1. Optimize the Use of Eevee for Real-Time Rendering

Eevee handles real-time rendering in Blender and version 4.4 further enhanced its performance. The following suggestions will optimize your utilization of Eevee in Blender.

A. Use the Right Lighting Setup

- **HDRI Lighting**: To generate lifelike natural lighting use HDRI because its easy configuration saves time and effort. Change the HDRI image strength in World settings to suit your scene requirements.
- **Limit Lights**: Multiple light sources decrease rendering speed on Eevee effectively. Minimize the number of lights you use to save GPU processing

power. Place Light Probes like Irradiance Volumes to build lighting quality without raising the number of light objects you use.

B. Utilize Simplified Shaders

- **Shader Complexity**: Real-time rendering needs basic editing of our shader programs. Keep your shaders basic and avoid using detailed shader components including excessive surface reflections and light interactions.

- **Principled BSDF**: The Basic Shader with Principles delivers effective results in real-time rendering. You should use this shader type as your main tool since it offers both good appearance and efficient processing.

C. Enable Simplify Options for Faster Previews

- During previews turn on Simplify in the Render Properties panel to cut down scene complexity. Some options under Simplify include:
  - **Max Subdivision**: The maximum number of subdivided elements in a model should decrease to improve preview speed.

- o **Texture Size**: Decrease texture file sizes especially for viewports to improve performance.
- o **Disable Shadows**: Preview mode performs faster when you switch shadow effects off or reduce them from full strength.

2. Use Viewport Shading Optimization Features

The Viewport provides your workspace view while you create scenes and it needs to work effortlessly even in large-scene projects.

A. Switch to Material Preview Mode for Fast Feedback

- Utilizing Fabric See Mode lets you check fabric appearance in Eevee without requiring a total rendered scene since of lower overhead. This mode speeds up workflow and facilitates visual plan requests compared to full Rendered Mode and gets to be exceptionally valuable for altering lighting setups.

B. Use the Viewport Samples Setting

- Lower the number of tests shown when rendering within the inspecting settings. You may get fast input together with your viewports whereas keeping the visualization quality great sufficient.

C. Turn Off Unnecessary Overlays

- Debilitate the graphical components you once in a while utilize amid viewport route to create Blender render more rapidly. These interface features utilize up CPU control so disabling them makes a difference real-time navigation work speedier.

3. Optimize Scene Complexity for Real-Time Rendering

To realize real-time rendering you wish to alter the level of detail and shock the framework. Bringing down polygon tallies and protest numbers additionally disentangling surfaces makes a difference make real-time Blender rendering run easily.

A. Reduce Polycounts

- **Decimate Modifier**: Utilize the Pulverize Modifier to lower the polygon tally of models when these objects require less points of interest and will not show up in close-up sees.

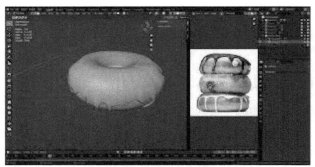
Reduce Polycounts

- **Simplify Meshes**: Lower the work detail on objects that don't show up near to the camera. Blender LOD strategies will switch between work resolutions that depend on camera remove.

B. Use Instancing

- **Instance Objects**: Working with numerous objects gets to be more effective through instancing since it diminishes memory utilize and boosts processing speed. Rather than making numerous copy objects utilize instancing with randomization controls.

C. Use Baking for High-Detail Assets

- Use the artwork delineations of lighting designs instep of doing costly computations during transfer. This strategy diminishes the ought to perform calculations when the program is running to supply way better spilling quality.

4. Reduce Reflection and Refraction Costs

Reflections and refractions burden the performance of live gameplay programs. These performance-improvement strategies help you preserve realism in your projects:

A. Limit Reflection and Refraction Effects

- **Reflection Probes**: You can achieve wider reflected surfaces by adding Reflection Cubemaps probes that replace individual surface reflection and refraction calculations. You can choose to freeze retrieved data by baking it or switch to update it directly in real time.

- **Screen-Space Reflections (SSR)**: Screen-Space Reflections help Eevee show realistic reflections but also consume more valuable resources. Lower SSR quality or raise the ray step limit to reach the right performance-to-image quality balance.

B. Use Reflection and Refraction Caching

- When working with reflective objects that need to depict reflections well Eevee supports caching these reflections. In World Properties select Bake

Reflection Cubemaps as an option to create pre-made reflections of set areas.

5. Leverage the Power of GPU for Faster Rendering

The Eevee real-time rendering mode uses all available GPU resources. Adjust both Blender tools and machine settings to achieve excellent rendering outcomes.

A. Use GPU for Rendering

- Set your device preference for rendering and viewport to use your GPU. You will find this option under Preferences > System. The real-time rendering of large scenes needs this option since CPUs deliver graphics poorly against the powerful GPU technology.

B. GPU Settings

- **Tile Size**: When working with GPU rendering turn up your tile size to 256 pixels per tile for better GPU functionality. Bigger tiles work faster but raise memory and CPU power needs.

C. Reduce GPU Memory Usage

- **Texture Compression**: Texture compression helps decrease memory use particularly when dealing with detailed texture files. Lower texture size settings in real-time work better especially in the Viewport because the GPU has fewer memory limits.

- **Texture Size**: Diminish the surface estimate in real-time Viewport mode to form beyond any doubt your GPU memory remains available.

6. Use the New Post-Processing Effects in Blender 4.4

The 4.4 adaptation of Blender lets you include unused post-processing impacts to Eevee and Cycles renders to improve the picture quality without abating down the rendering prepare. These impacts incorporate:

A. Bloom and Depth of Field (DOF)

- **Bloom**: Light regions have to be have blossoming included to mellow their appearance. Keep track of the threshold settings since they decide the brightness yield.
- **Depth of Field**: Utilize Profundity of Field to make a cinematic appearance in your scene by mimicking camera focal point highlights. Alter your center separate and alter the opening setting for idealize render comes about. Keep a adjust between depth-of-field impact quality and performance speed.

Depth of Field

B. Ambient Occlusion and Screen-Space Reflections

- Set Encompassing Impediment (AO) on in Eevee mode to form protest shading look superior and appear appropriate shadow contact. Turning down the surrounding impediment separate will speed up rendering.

- Turn on Screen-Space Reflections (SSR) within the scene for progressed reflection precision. To optimize execution whereas keeping up picture quality lower the greatest number of beam testing steps.

7. Conclusion

Eevee's real-time rendering control in Blender 4.4 has expanded but you would like optimization steps to coordinate this control with extraordinary quality. Accurately controlling lighting plans combined with materials determination and legitimate equipment setup brings you top-quality real-time execution. Apply these recommendations to your work schedule to create and look at quick extend comes about in genuine time.

CHAPTER FIVE
ANIMATION & RIGGING
Keyframe Animation in Blender 4.4

Keyframe animation is the fundamental process used in Blender to empower models and animation through time. You create smooth and advanced animations in Blender by setting important motion positions during different time points. The keyframe controls in Blender 4.4 have new updates that make it simpler to move and control different objects and camera elements in your projects. In this section we will show you basic keyframe animation methods in Blender 4.4 plus efficient ways to work more effectively.

1. What is Keyframe Animation?

You place defined keyframes throughout selected moments during animation. You set up keyframes to hold the essential attributes of each object like its place in space, angle, size, and surface traits. Blender uses the keyframe data to create smooth transitioning frames between each defined position.

- **Keyframe**: To set keyframe animation you specify object attributes at predefined time points known as marks.
- **Interpolation**: Blender creates gradual frame movements between keyframes through automatic calculations using different interpolation methods (linear and cubic).

2. Setting Up Keyframe Animation in Blender 4.4

Take after this simple method to begin including and altering keyframe liveliness utilizing Blender 4.4.

A. Inserting Keyframes

1. **Select an Object**: Select your activity element by selecting it from the show window.
2. **Set the Timeline**: Move the Timeline playhead marker to outline number one on the foot screen.
3. **Modify the Object**: Modify the object's highlights you want to energize when moving it around, turning it, scaling it or altering its surface color.
4. **Insert the Keyframe**:
   - Select Insert Keyframe by right-clicking on the changed object property.
   - You can use I to access the Insert Keyframe menu in the 3D Viewport and select which

property to update including Location, Rotation, Scale, and more.

5. **Move to Another Frame**: Rephrase your edits on the other chosen frame number 20 then update the changes.

6. **Insert Another Keyframe**: Use the right-click menu or press key I to create a second keyframe entry.

Inserting Keyframes

The shifts between both keyframes emerge automatically through Blender's timing feature.

B. Understanding the Timeline

- **Keyframe Markers**: The timeline indicates keyframe changes through yellow diamonds. These diamonds mark all positions in time when the object properties receive specific updates.

130

- **Playhead**: The moving blue bar helps you view which frame is currently displayed on the timeline.

Understanding the Timeline

C. Scrubbing Through the Timeline

- **Scrubbing**: You can test animation movement by sliding the playhead across the timeline. The timeline shows you transformations in the object during its specified key positions.

- **Playback**: Press the Spacebar key to begin and pause your animation while in the Blender 4.4 workflow. Spacebar plays the animation in real-time either from the beginning or from the present frame.

3. Editing Keyframes in Blender 4.4

You can adjust your keyframe animation without difficulty in Blender 4.4's system.

A. Moving Keyframes

1. Point to the keyframe you need to modify in the Timeline and the selection will turn red.

131

2. Using G on your keyboard lets you select a keyframe and move it to another time position.

3. Click your mouse button once to position the keyframe at the selected frame.

B. Deleting Keyframes

1. To delete a keyframe choose it by right-clicking on its entry in the timeline.

2. Choose Delete or Press X to erase the selected keyframe.

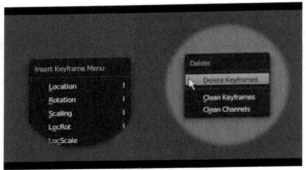

Deleting Keyframes

C. Adjusting Keyframe Interpolation

The object motion between keyframes gets defined by Blender through the use of interpolation. The program preference for Blender is to use Bezier curves to create smooth motion but you can select alternative forms of interpolation.

132

1. **Graph Editor**: Launch the Graph Editor using the editor type dropdown.
2. When you open the Graph Editor you will notice a graphic showing how the property changes across its keyframes.
3. Choose the keyframes you need to modify.
4. You can access the Set Keyframe Interpolation menu by pressing the T key.
5. Choose an interpolation type:
    o **Linear**: Constant speed between keyframes.
    o **Bezier**: The Bezier setting produces smooth transitions that mimic natural movement effectively.
    o **Constant**: Holds the value until the next keyframe (no interpolation).
    o **Exponential** or **Sine**: The exponential or sine interaction provides new ways to create bouncing or overshooting motion motions.

D. Keyframe Editing in the Dope Sheet

1. **Dope Sheet**: The Dope Sheet serves as a tool to help users view and handle keyframes through a timeline system.
2. On the Dope Sheet you can view all scene keyframes for different objects side by side so you

133

can enhance keyframe timing while working on several keys at once easily.

3. Right-click to pick and place keyframes within the Dope Sheet operations just as you do using the Timeline tool.

4. Advanced Keyframe Animation Features

Blender 4.4 technology improves how users work with keyframe animation tools at an advanced level.

A. Auto Keying

By default Android users will get keyframes whenever they change object settings in Auto Keying mode. The auto keying feature saves you time because it sets up keyframes by itself as you make object changes.

1. Click the red button next to the Timeline to activate Auto Keying. You can also switch it on by pressing Shift + Space.
2. As you adjust position rotation or scale of any object Blender automatically sets a keyframe at the active frame.

B. Keyframe Extrapolation

Through extrapolation you can create a seamless animation by extending the frames which began at the last keyframe.

1. Choose the end keyframes in your animation.
2. Click right with your computer mouse to access the Extrapolate command for motion extension. The animation extends through choice between three extrapolation types: Constant, Linear and Bezier.

C. Action Editor and NLA Editor

The Blender 4.4 software package features the Action Editor and Nonlinear Animation (NLA) Editor for building advanced animations. Multi-animation control becomes possible through specialized tools in Blender 4.4 which provide flexible animation management features:

- **Action Editor**: Action Editor provides a system for developing as well as managing independent animations which includes character motions and camera movements etc.

Action Editor

- **NLA Editor**: A NLA Editor tool enables users to stack various documented actions together (such as character animations which include walking combined with jumping interspersed with idle movements).

NLA Editor

D. Motion Paths for Animation Preview

Visual representations of object movements exist through Motion Paths within the timeline space. Previewing complicated animations becomes simpler using this function.

1. Choose the object which needs previewing from the available selection.
2. From the panel view of Object Properties select the Motion Paths subsection.
3. Running the Calculate function creates motion path visualization that displays the object trajectory through animation space.

5. Tips for Smooth Keyframe Animation

- **Use F-Curves for Precision**: From the Graph Editor interface use F-Curves to conduct manual adjustments that smooth out and control animation curves.

- **Easing In/Out**: The natural flow of your animations becomes possible when you implement easing effects at either the beginning (easing in) or ending (easing out) parts of your keyframes.

- **Animate in Small Increments**: Animation of keyframes should happen through incremental movements because you will need to modify each frame one by one.

- **Copying and Pasting Keyframes**: Selecting keyframes in the Dope Sheet or Graph Editor enables users to duplicate them using Ctrl+C then Ctrl+V which allows them to move these keyframes throughout the timeline.

- **Use the Timeline Markers**: Users should place Timeline Markers in their timeline to monitor essential stages during animation development.

6. Conclusion

The animation system in Blender 4.4 contains numerous tools and capabilities designed to produce refined complicated animations. Using fundamental understanding of keyframes and interpolation with Auto Keying and NLA advanced features enables users to animate objects cameras and materials easily. The keyframe animation tools in Blender provide users with versatile features which allow them to control animations for basic object movement and advanced character rigging.

Armatures & Rigging in Blender 4.4

A 3D model benefits from rigging through the development of an armature called skeleton that enables dynamic lifelike animation possibilities. The Blender program includes an armature system which functions as a bone structure that users use to control animations of characters and creatures and complex motions of mechanical objects. Your model function works better with rigging tools since it enables natural movements through realistic animation controls. The rigging workflow of Blender 4.4 received additional enhancements through new tools which improve both rig creation and management.

This part instructs you about basic concepts related to Armatures along with Rigging features in Blender version 4.4.

1. Introduction to Armatures

An armature exists as a group of bones which operates to regulate both model movement and body deformation. The bones function as the core structural elements within animated characters or objects because they provide the necessary base for animation.

- **Bone**: Every armature contains one bone element which represents individual skeletal parts. Every bone within an armature controls specific areas of the mesh together with specific movement capabilities.
- **Pose Mode**: Users use Pose Mode to move the bones within the armature framework for animation purpose.

2. Creating an Armature

A. Adding an Armature

1. **Add an Armature**: The beginning step to create an armature starts when you navigate to the 3D Viewport to press Shift + A before selecting Armature followed by Single Bone. The addition of this single bone places it in the center of the entire scene area.

2. **Edit the Armature**: When the armature reaches creation stage users should switch to Edit Mode through selecting the armature followed by pressing Tab. The Edit Mode allows users to create and modify their bones through the process of adding and removing along with replicating positions.

   o **Extruding Bones**: Bones should be extruded by pressing E on selected bones followed by proper bone placement according to requirements. The same extrusion technique allows you to generate additional armature components such as spine, limbs or finger bones.

- o **Moving Bones**: You can pick any bone from your object and press G to effectively move it. Commands R and S help users to rotate and scale bones in the system.

3. **Naming Bones**: Each bone needs a rational identification system starting with "upper_arm.L" for left upper arm and "lower_leg.R" for right lower leg to maintain control of your armature when creating complex rigs.

B. Bone Hierarchy

Almost all bones exist in an hierarchical parent-child system. A parent bone establishes rules for the comparative motion of connected child bones. For example:

- Managing the movement of connected bones requires the upper arm bone to function as the parent element which guides the lower arm bone.
- All bones in the armature should have their root bone as their parent bone.

To set up bone hierarchy:

1. **Select a Bone**: A user should first access Edit Mode before they choose the child bone.

2. **Parenting**: A parent relationship can be set with the press of Ctrl + P. Please select from available parenting options to determine bone behavior (Connected or Keep Offset).

3. Skinning (Weight Painting)

Next step for armature development requires binding the created structure to your 3D model. The rigging procedure also known as skinning requires selecting each bone for weight assignment that determines their influence range over mesh segments.

Skinning (Weight Painting)

A. Adding a Mesh to the Armature

1. **Parent the Mesh to the Armature**: Select the mesh after that choose Shift + Select the armature before proceeding to press Ctrl + P with Automatic Weights enabled. Select Ctrl + P and choose With Automatic Weights from the dialogue box. The mesh will receive automatic weighting from Blender which depends on how closely the mesh exists to bone structures.

2. **Weight Painting**: The mesh parenting process ends by switching to Weight Paint Mode to refine how each bone affects the mesh through painting.

   o In Weight Paint Mode the bones appear in three distinct coloring schemes: red for full influence, green for partial influence and blue for no influence.

   o You can adjust bone influence on selected mesh vertices by painting directly onto the bones in the interface. You can adjust the Weight value inside the Tools panel.

B. Editing Weights

1. **Automatic Weights**: The Automatic Weights system from Blender delivers satisfactory weight results for basic rigging yet enables users to

enhance control when they manually edit weight values.

2. **Paint Weights**: Weight Paint Mode allows artists to directly paint bone influences on mesh portions through corresponding parts of the animated body.

   o **Add/Remove Weights**: The Weight Paint Mode provides Add and Subtract brushes which users can use for custom weight adjustment on selected areas of the mesh.

   o **Smooth Weights**: In the transition regions between bones (shoulder and hip areas) you should apply the Smooth brush to achieve even weight distribution.

4. Posing the Armature

After completing the armature setup along with its skinning process you can start animating or posing.

A. Pose Mode

1. **Entering Pose Mode**: Begin by selecting the armature object while using Ctrl + Tab to enter the Pose mode.

2. **Manipulating Bones**: Pose Mode allows manipulation of bones in a manner similar to Edit

Mode while the main purpose remains character. Payment instead of structural bone changes.

- o **Grab**: Press G to move bones.
- o **Rotate**: Press R to rotate bones.
- o **Scale**: Press S to scale bones.

3. **Mirroring Poses**: You can apply pose mirroring to symmetrical characters (for instance human figures) through the X-Axis Mirror option in the Tools Shelf. You can find X-Axis Mirror enabled under the Pose tab of the Tool Shelf during Pose Mode to achieve automatic bone transformation mirroring.

5. Rigging for Animation

You can begin animating your character after positioning the armature while having the figure in proper pose. Certain basic rigging techniques will advance your animation practice as follows:

A. IK (Inverse Kinematics) vs FK (Forward Kinematics)

- **Forward Kinematics (FK)**: The process of Forward Kinematics (FK) allows you to move bones through animating the parent towards the child one (shoulder rotation to animate arm movement). The method works best for animating human body parts starting from the arms and legs.

- **Inverse Kinematics (IK)**: The Inverse Kinematics (IK) system allows you to position a body part through its end effector and the system will generate bone positions to reach the desired effector. IK (Inverse Kinematics) is essential for maintaining contact between rigid body parts such as feet when they remain on the floor.

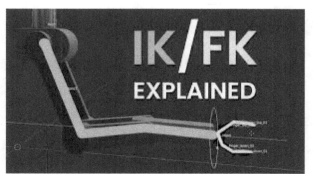

Inverse Kinematics vs Forward Kinematics

To set up IK:

1. **Add an IK Constraint**: Select the bone you want to control in Pose Mode (for example the foot) after which you should navigate to the Bone Constraints tab.

2. **Set the Target**: The IK target bone selection (often an arm or leg) should be set for control of all linked bones through the target settings configuration.

B. Rigging Facial Animation

When making facial animations you should establish a facial rig through bones to create both lip synchronization and facial expressions. You possess two options to create face animation through either using facial bones that target specific areas or implementing dynamic shape key elements.

- **Shape Keys**: The technology of shape keys serves to modify mesh deformation during facial expressions such as smiling.
- **Facial Rig with Bones**: The face rig system uses bones to control how the jaw, eyebrows and mouth move during body animations.

6. Rigging with Add-ons

The update 4.4 from Blender software includes top-tier add-ons that help you rig and animate faster:

- **Rigify**: The powerful rigify tool generates automatic rigs for human and animal characters very fast. The software offers basic character rig templates for easy modification based on your character needs.
- **Auto-Rig Pro**: The costed Auto-Rig Pro features advanced rigging tools that let users create body rigging efficiently and provide automatic facial setup capabilities.

Rigify

To use Rigify:

1. To use Rigify first enable the Add-on by choosing Preferences then selecting the Add-ons tab.

148

2. Create a human rig base through Armature > Human (Meta-Rig).

3. Adjust the rig properties then begin the final armature creation through Generate Rig.

7. Conclusion

To form reasonable movements Blender 4.4 clients require the total fixing prepare for scenes and figures. The key to building tried and true character rigs lies in learning armature plan also weight portray nearby the nuts and bolts of character pose creation also IK/FK control and progressed facial controller execution. Blender's effective toolset particularly Rigify upgrades fix era which makes a difference handle complex setups speedier. Classes in fixing are principal for movement experts who work on computer diversions and visual impacts whereas making distinctive 3D models.

Grease Pencil Updates in Blender 4.4

Blender users can make 2D animations and freehand drawings directly on the 3D workplane using Grease Pencil tools. Using Grease Pencil and Blender tools artists can create sketch ideas, animated 2D art, and full 2D characters while working in the 3D space. Blender 4.4 gives Grease

Pencil users better 2D animation tools with new updates that let them make complex drawings smoothly. This section explains the new functions and enhancements for Grease Pencil in Blender 4.4 release.

1. Grease Pencil Workflow Enhancements

The most recent Blender 4.4 upgrade rearranges the Oil Pencil apparatuses so specialists can draw 2D movements superior and quicker. The program presently grants improved drawing execution whereas making it less difficult to construct and control layers over 2D illustrations in 3D space.

A. Improved Drawing Tools

1. **New Brush Engine**: With Blender 4.4 the program offers a much better brush motor for Grace Pencil work. The overhaul moves forward how you control brush strokes by giving moment response to weight changes whereas making moves stream way better and letting your drawings feel normal.

2. **Brush Dynamics**: You'll alter brush breadth thickness speed relations with unused brush highlights that screen weight and movement speed. Clients can produce more complex work of art since

the modern highlight gifts movable brush alternatives.

3. **Smoothing and Stabilization**: Drawing execution can presently advantage from a unused stabilizing work that diminishes trembles and makes sharp strokes. The smoothing highlight empowers clients to upgrade the brushstrokes to attain smoother and cleaner outlines.

B. Stroke and Path Improvements

1. **Stroke Editing**: The new Blender 4.4 version offers superior control when altering strokes so you'll alter their geometric shapes. You'll be able adjust stroke ebb and flow and thickness furthermore other qualities in each made stroke.

2. **Vectorization**: Vectorization includes a modern apparatus for clients to alter Grease Pencil strokes into graphical ways that clients can alter and quicken. You'll be able presently move between 2D and 3D movement instruments without changes since vectorized strokes carry on as conventional 2D activity components.

2. Layer Management Improvements

The added layer administration apparatuses presently makes it less demanding to work on complicated Grease Pencil activitys. The framework permits you to handle numerous vivified layers proficiently by altering which layers display and where they fit within the progression.

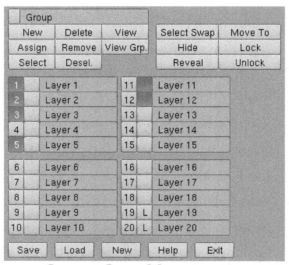

Improve Layer Management

A. Layer Visibility and Locking

1. **Layer Visibility**: You'll presently toggle the deceivability of each layer within the Grease Pencil Protest properties for more multitasking in working with numerous layers.

152

2. **Lock Layers**: It is presently conceivable to lock layers, so that in the event that you attempt to alter them by accident, the layer remains unaltered. . This feature is particularly handy when you have layers that are already locked or you want to keep them unchanged and this while working over other layers.

B. Enhanced Layer Management in the Timeline

1. **Timeline Layer Control**: Blender 4.4 Enhances Grease Pencil layer integration in the Timeline. You can now easily scrub through various layers, a preview view specific parts of your animation, and your layer visibility toggle directly in the Timeline.

2. **Auto-merge Layers**: When drawing or animating, Grease Pencil layers can be now auto-merged, offering a smooth transition between the layers and working on overlapping or interconnected scenes.

3. Animation & Timing Updates

Blender 4.4 provides several 2D animation system enhancements to Grease Pencil, enabling smoother, more detailed 2D animation took by kind of workflows.

A. Improved Keyframe System

1. **Keyframe Editing**: The keyframe system for Grease Pencil has been improved for more flexibility with editing animation. Keyframe control has become more precise, more possibilities to customise interpolation curves, and switch between frame-by-frame & keyframe-based animation ways are now all available.

2. **Frame-by-Frame Animation**: The frame-by-frame animation system has been Enhanced for better responsiveness, smoother animations and smoother transitions between frames. The way to conveniently browse between frames and time adjustment has been improved, making the animation process faster and easier.

3. **Onion Skinning**: Improved onion skinning in Query 4.4 nails animators while both preceding and following frames are more visible. You can now control the number of frames displayed with the onion skinning tool and the level of its opacity; this should help to make your 2D animation refining process more efficient.

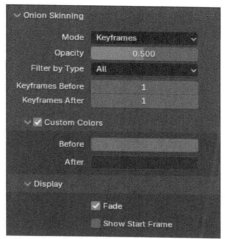

Onion Skinning

B. Auto-Interpolation of Frames

Blender 4.4 include a new auto interpolation system, which automates the generation of missing frames for Grease Pencil animations, helping the animation procedure. This comes in handy for artists who wish to roughly turn off the animation and then improve it later on.

4. Grease Pencil and 3D Integration

Blender has always been able to combine 2D animation with 3D objects and that ability has been further strengthened in version 4.4.

A. 3D Space Drawing

1. **Depth and Perspective Control**: Directly draw in 3D space w/ full depth and perspective control. This gives the toolmaker for 2D objects, in the 3D environment, more flexibility when animated.

2. **Grease Pencil Objects in 3D Viewport**: Viewport view in 3D allows improved integration for examination and alteration of Grease Collection objects, including superior camera convenience and perspectives. This allows animations of 2D sketches within a 3D scene, which is required for mixed media projects.

B. Grease Pencil in 3D Shaders

1. **Material Integration**: Grease Pencil lines now blend in perfectly with Blender's 3D materials, and shaders. You can also use Shaders, Textures and Lighting to Grease Pencil strokes for a more creative control on the look of your 2D animations in 3D scenes.

2. **3D Grease Pencil Effects**: Blender 4.4 enables users to add 3D- based effects such as shading, lighting and texturing on top of Grease Pencil strokes and brings 2D and 3D animation and styling closer.

5. Grease Pencil Materials & Textures

The Grease Pencil material system in Blender 4.4 gives more control over the visual appearance of your strokes, from solid fills to intricate texture.

A. Texture Painting for Grease Pencil

1. **Texture Mapping**: Users of Grease Pencil strokes can specifically include surfaces through Texture Mapping which comes about in painterly appearance as well as complex features counting angle designs and aesthetic impacts.

2. **Brush Textures**: Brush Textures allow Blender 4.4 users to draw Grease Pencil strokes with numerous textures chosen by brush types leading to shifted portray styles from quick draws to expand outlines.

B. Material Layering

1. **Material Layers**: Users now have the capacity to stack different materials inside each Oil Pencil protest which empowers them to draw complex strokes. Diverse drawing segments counting traces and fills nearby highlights can naturally select interesting materials and impacts since of this upgrade.

2. **Color Control**: Improved color control functions in Grease Pencil materials donate clients way better control over stroke colors beside superior slope and transparency alterations. The mixing modes combined with murkiness controls permit clients to produce progressed visual impacts through their strokes.

6. Performance & Usability Improvements

Blender 4.4 generates improved execution for Oil Pencil especially amid operation with significant complex projects.

A. Performance Optimization

1. **Faster Stroke Drawing**: Stroke drawing within Grease Pencil presently runs faster notwithstanding of the complexity level of scenes that contain numerous thousands of strokes. Computer program clients encounter faster and smoother execution amid drawing operations as well as altering and enlivened work since of later speed overhauls.

2. **Viewport Performance**: The viewport performance received an upgrade in Blender 4.4 which conveys more quick render yield nearby made strides client interface smoothness when working with Oil Pencil

objects. The overhauled framework empowers illustrators to work with speed through both high-definition strokes and complex scenes.

B. User Interface Updates

1. **UI Refinements**: The 4.4 release of Blender implements numerous refinements to its Grease Pencil client interface hence clients can get to highlights more effectively. Brushes and materials in expansion to movement controls have gotten unused board organization making them open with more noteworthy speed.

2. **Grease Pencil Brushes & Settings Presets**: Grease Pencil Brushes & Settings Presets represents a new system which enables better brush preset and settings management thereby facilitating more efficient customization of tools for particular animation work.

7. Conclusion

The latest updates for Grease Pencil tools within Blender 4.4 provide multiple enhancements that simplify complex animation production between two-dimensional and three-dimensional environments for illustrators and animators. The range of new features in Blender 4.4 including improved drawing tools as well as better layer control, 3D capabilities and system optimizations allows artists to produce superior animated and illustrative work. The upgraded Grease Pencil features in Blender 4.4 allow anyone to realize their animation concepts through traditional 2D animations and 2D characters in 3D environments and mixed-media projects.

CHAPTER SIX
SIMULATIONS & EFFECTS
Fluid, Cloth & Particle Systems in Blender 4.4

Blender 4.4 addresses the simulation systems with numerous updates which simplify the creation of authentic effects that involve fluids and cloth alongside particles. The simulation systems in Blender enable users to produce virtual representations of natural occurrences including water movement and fabric simulation and complex particle movements for visual effects and animation purposes. Readers will find an overview of current improvements in Blender's Fluid, Cloth and Particle Systems featured within this analysis.

1. Fluid Simulation Updates

Fluid simulation through Blender enables users to generate authentic fluid behavior including water and oil as well as different substances that react to objects in scenes.

A. Mantaflow Enhancements

MantaFlow from Blender continued its development path throughout Blender 4.4 after its initial release in earlier versions. The Mantaflow system in Blender manages both fluid and smoke simulations while the developers improved its performance to provide better quality results more quickly.

1. **Faster Fluid Simulations**: Blender 4.4 now simulates fluids rapidly especially in scenarios that handle extensive scenes. The adaptive domain feature enables fluid simulation domains to change size automatically based on simulation requirements which shortens the time needed for computations.

Faster Fluid Simulations

2. **Improved Mesh Output**: The outcome mesh of fluid simulations features enhanced quality and accuracy that results in superior mesh conversion from fluids to surface meshes. The new mesh refinement tool upgrades mesh quality through

162

improvement of fluid surface realism by eliminating artifacts.

3. **Viscosity and Surface Tension**: The latest Blender version 4.4 introduces enhancements for users to precisely control both fluid viscosity levels and surface tension parameters during simulation sequences.. Users can accomplish more point by point control over liquid thickness whereas deciding its surface engagement with objects and discuss.

4. **Multithreading for Fluid Simulations**: The expansion of full multithreading bolster for liquid reenactments amplifies the speed of handling amid times when numerous processors are dynamic. Complex simulations experience improved performance while resources become used efficiently through this feature.

2. Cloth Simulation Updates

Realistic fabrics and clothing motion derives from essential cloth simulation operations. The most up to date Blender adaptation 4.4 provides major updates to its cloth reenactment capabilities which makes more dependable execution nearby way better interface ease of use and quicker reactions.

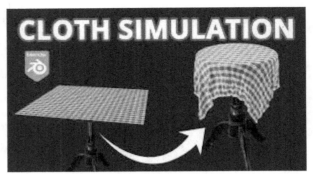
Cloth Simulation Updates

A. Cloth Collision Improvements

1. **Improved Collision Detection**: Cloth simulation collision discovery has gotten a comprehensive advancement. Way better self-collision discovery capabilities have been actualized in Blender 4.4 so cloth materials associated without entering each other. The specific requirement becomes critical when working with various cloth pieces or objects during simulations.

2. **Friction and Bending Control**: New parameters for friction and bending stiffness in simulations enable users to control the way cloth objects react. New configuration options help generate authentic fabric movement behavior including resistant fabric materials which naturally slide over each other.

3. **Interactive Simulation Improvements**: The cloth simulation system now updates in real time as it reacts to objects to deliver improved interaction during editing and simulation of cloth behavior.

B. Cloth Simulation Performance Optimizations

1. **Performance Enhancements**: The cloth solver received improved performance optimization tools which bring both accelerated simulations and enhanced resource allocation. The system performs better during playback while delivering quick results especially when handling complex fabric movements.

2. **Wind and Airflow Simulation**: Wind and Airflow Simulation achieves new capabilities through the addition of these features in Blender 4.4 that allow users to apply wind effects on cloth objects. The Wind Force Field enhancement provides users with advanced tools to generate more natural cloth reactions under wind gusts and environmental airflow.

3. Particle System Updates

Blender implements its particle systems for creating natural effects that include fire simulation together with smoke and hair elements along with dust and other natural phenomena. Blender 4.4 enhances the particle system features with substantial updates that advance usability standards and increase authentic effects.

Particle System Updates

A. Hair and Fur Improvements

1. **Better Hair Simulation**: The hair simulation system received enhancements to develop precise behavior simulations for hair and fur. The natural behavior of hair and its reactions to other object collisions along with wind and gravity forces

166

achieves improved animator control in scene movements.

2. **Guided Hair Strands**: Blender 4.4 provides users with an option to apply guide structures through which hair strands may be created. Users have more control over initial hair shape and therefore better define how hair flows and responds to forces in the scene. The introduction of guides enables users to handle hair styling more easily for animation purposes.

3. **Hair and Particle Instancing**: The capability to employ hair particles for object instance applications received substantial improvement. Users achieve simpler creation of complex environments with effects including grass and forests through using hair particles for object instantiation.

B. Particle Dynamics & Interaction with Forces

1. **Advanced Force Fields**: In Blender 4.4 the advanced force field capabilities have been integrated into particle systems. The inclusion of turbulence with vortex and magnetic forces provides scene objects with enhanced control for

moving particles and their interaction patterns in the 4.4 version.

Force Fields

2. **Better Particle Collisions**: Particle systems now provide improved collision capabilities between their objects in relation to the other scene elements. Enhanced detection and interaction capabilities produce sophisticated particle behaviors that result in surface bounces and object attachment as well as trail generation through force interactions.

3. **Particle-Based Fluid Simulations**: The addition of Particle-Based Fluid Simulations enables users to work with mixed simulations of fluid and particulate systems. The ability of particles to represent liquids emerges when using them for understanding fluid dynamics which enables splash

effects together with dripping behaviors and droplet movement.

4. Real-Time Simulation and Performance Enhancements

Merged in Blender version 4.4 is an update that increases real-time performance of simulation elements including fluid and cloth together with particles thus allowing more interactive viewport operations.

A. Simulation Cache Improvements

1. **Faster Cache Previews**: The creators improved the cache system that manages fluid and cloth and particle simulation previews to deliver speedier previews. Simulations become faster to view in the viewport without requiring users to bake the entire simulation whenever a modification occurs.

2. **Incremental Baking**: The introduction of incremental baking in Blender 4.4 enables users to update specific simulation frames that changed thus shortening the whole baking process duration particularly for time-consuming large and complex simulations.

B. Adaptive Sampling

1. **Adaptive Sampling for Fluids**: Blender 4.4 includes adaptive sampling technology which uses detailed fluid calculations solely in moving fluid structures and areas of fundamental interaction. The new system optimizes overall performance while maintaining complete details for essential regions in simulated areas.

2. **Cloth Simulation Adaptive Detail**: The complexity of cloth simulations determines how much detail the adaptive detail system generates during calculations. Simpler cloth simulations experience faster performance while the efficient resource allocation targets detailed areas of the simulation.

5. New Tools for Particle and Fluid Visual Effects

Blender 4.4 provides multiple new tools to enable artists in developing intricate particle and fluid effects which serve animation and visual storytelling needs best.

A. Particle-Driven Fluid Effects

1. **Fluid Mesh from Particles**: Using Fluid Mesh from Particles in Blender 4.4 transforms particle objects into fluid mesh elements which improve the

fluid realism between fluid particles and their surface. The system proves valuable for producing realistic fluid movements that occur during liquid splashes and waves and dripping actions.

2. **Splash and Foam Generation**: The simulation tools provide designers with enhanced capabilities to produce both splashes and foam patterns in fluid simulations. The new system allows dynamic emission of particles through fluid dynamics traits that enable interactions with other objects to generate authentic results.

B. Volumetric Fluid Effects

1. **Volumetric Fluid Simulation**: The software update Blender 4.4 enables users to deliver voluminous impacts when running liquid recreations. The expansion of volume capabilities to liquids empowers designers to create different impacts whereas working with thick fluids, mist or fog highlights in liquid reenactments. 3D environment reenactments of fluids and gasses gotten to be more reasonable since of this highlight.

6. Conclusion

Blender 4.4 delivered essential advancements to fluid, cloth and particle systems which resulted in improved reality levels and enhanced simulation speed together with expanded system flexibility. Users now have greater control over enhanced performance tools and intuitive interfaces which enables them to build advanced visual effects for animations and VFX as well as interactive media. The latest Blender 4.4 release presents a complete collection of simulation features that allow artists and animators to make their scenes more authentic through the use of natural-looking water, fabric, hair and particle effects.

Dynamic Paint & Smoke in Blender 4.4

The new Blender 4.4 improves the functional capabilities of both Dynamic Paint and Smoke Simulation tools that enable 3D users to generate physical interaction-based visual elements. Objects in Blender can now use Dynamic Paint to interact with paint and texture surfaces and Smoke Simulations to generate authentic gaseous special effects which include smoke and fire elements. Such systems function best as visual effects tools to boost the realistic quality of animated content. The section showcases the recent updates within Dynamic Paint and Smoke features implemented in Blender 4.4.

1. Dynamic Paint Updates

Dynamic Paint of Blender enables users to render surface effects including footprints by applying textures that stem from object-object interactions for producing water-inspired effects, blood stains among others. The new Blender 4.4 release provides multiple features which improve the usability along with the realism of Dynamic Paint functionality.

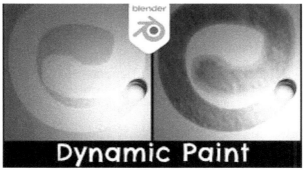
Dynamic Paint Updates

A. Surface Type Enhancements

1. **Wet Map and Dry Map Improvements**: A new system update in Blender 4.4 enhances the capabilities for producing wet and dry maps. Now the wet map reacts in a more life-like fashion and

smoothly combines with the dry map surface type. Using this option produces realistic changes in object appearance due to liquid affecting them such as paint and water. Real-time simulations perform better using the dry/wet system of the application.

2. **Enhanced Surface Effects**: Dynamic Paint provides greater capabilities in surface displacement and texture painting through improved enhancement. The precision of surface deformation after painting or interaction creates enhanced realistic effects when making effects such as mud, footprints or water puddles.

B. Multiple Brush Types

Dynamic Paint surfaces in Blender 4.4 receive new multiple brush types which operate differently on Dynamic Paint surface areas. Users can create their own custom brushes that have defined effects suitable for painting various dynamic surfaces including liquid flow and splashes and special effects.

1. **Brush Customization**: Users gain full customization over brush behavior through capabilities to modify brush shape alongside size

and hardness and texturing features that control paint application and interaction dynamics.

2. **Interactive Brushes**: Interactive brushes in Blender 4.4 have better responsiveness through pressure-sensitive and rotating brushes that let users create realistic effects including wetness and footprints and surface wear.

C. Support for Multiple Dynamic Paint Layers

The latest Blender 4.4 version adds the capability to apply several dynamic paint layers simultaneously to a single object. The system enables flexible painting methods by letting different paint types (consisting of wet dry and dirty materials etc.) exist singularly for individual manipulation.

- **Layer Blending**: You can create advanced appearance effects through blending your multiple dynamic paint layers. The software allows an object to possess multiple paint layers with independent functions as separate entities.

D. Real-Time Feedback and Performance Enhancements

1. **Faster Simulations**: The Dynamic Paint system delivers improved performance for faster

simulations which applies especially to big complex simulation-based scenarios. The integration process improves the paint baking system allowing for more responsive real-time feedback together with accelerated simulation periods.

2. **Viewport Previews**: Blender 4.4 enables realtime viewport previews in Dynamic Paint that lets artists view their surface paint effects directly within the viewport interface. The preview functions offer immediate visual results that minimize the amount of time needed for repetitive baking processes.

2. Smoke Simulation Updates

Through Manta flow as its main solver Blender provides a smoke simulation tool that enables users to create realistic effects involving smoke and fire. The latest version of Blender 4.4 delivers numerous critical upgrades which enhance both the realistic appearance and simplified usage of smoke effects.

Smoke Simulation Updates

A. Smoke Density and Viscosity Enhancements

1. **Smoke Density Control**: With Blender 4.4 users gain better capabilities to set smoke density values. Users now have better control to simulate dense realistic smoke over time while determining how the material spreads.

2. **Viscosity and Temperature Variations**: Users benefit from additional viscosity options that allow them to model both thick emitter gases like fog and thin transparent smoke in Blender 4.4. Smoke interactions with objects and temperature sources become more authentic through improved temperature control specifications in Blender 4.4..

B. Improved Smoke Interaction with Objects

1. **Smoke & Cloth Interactions**: The new Blender 4.4 implements better smoke and cloth interaction

capabilities. Smoke passes naturally through cloth materials in Blender 4.4 which allows users to perform more believable smoke-pattern interactions with wind or fabrics.

2. **Object Collision for Smoke**: Blender 4.4 provides users with advanced ways to manage how smoke behaves when objects collide with it. The interactions of Smoke through its contact with different surfaces have become more lifelike since it follows contact with and avoidance of hard and soft obstacles.

C. Fire and Smoke Combination

1. **Fire-Specific Smoke Control**: The procedure of fire-smoke simulation produces different smoke behavior patterns than standard heating methods leading to improved accuracy in smoke dispersion near fire points.

2. **Smoke from Multiple Sources**: The Blender 4.4 update enhances the way different smoke and fire sources interact with one another when active in the scene. Using additional emitters allows the smoke particles to blend naturally which results in effects suitable for depicting various scenes that require

multiple heat sources like explosions and extensive fires.

D. Performance Enhancements for Smoke Simulations

1. **Adaptive Smoke Resolution**: Retinal density in Blender 4.4 adapts to smoke simulations by escalating resolution in relevant regions specifically where turbulence or combustion exists but lowers resolution throughout other unimportant sections for enhanced performance. The method of fire-smoke recreation produces diverse smoke behavior designs than standard warming strategies driving to progressed exactness in smoke scattering close fire focuses.

2. **Multithreaded Performance**: The Blender 4.4 update improves the way distinctive smoke and fire sources connected with one another when dynamic within the scene. Utilizing extra emitters permits the smoke particles to mix actually which comes about in impacts appropriate for portraying different scenes that require different warm sources like blasts and broad fires.

E. Real-Time Smoke Simulation Feedback

1. **Viewport Smoke Previews**: Blendter 4.4 provides viewport preview of smoke effects which updates in real time so you can modify settings during live observation. Users will now receive better quality visualizations that show both smoke density levels and fire effects while working in the design space.

2. **Smoke Visualization with Volume Shaders**: Volume Shaders enhance the display of smoke in Blender 4.4 by enabling better visualization which produces authentic results for viewport and final outcomes. The updated lighting system brings natural conditions combined with shading effects that enable smoke to interact properly with light elements.

3. Smoke and Dynamic Paint Integration

Blender 4.4 enhances the association between Dynamic Paint and smoke simulations so clients can achieve modern intuitively impacts.

1. **Smoke Painting**: Your Blender models will presently produce smoke outflows all through their intelligent when they utilize the Energetic Paint functionality. The software provides features which

mimic smoke damage to walls and floors when these materials encounter smoke.

2. **Dynamic Paint as Smoke Source**: With Blender 4.4 users can employ objects designated as Dynamic Paint surfaces to create smoke emission through the new feature Dynamic Paint as Smoke Source. A surface decorated with wet paint will produce smoke during its drying process which enables digital evaporation and other environmental effects.

4. Conclusion

The latest Blender 4.4 software update implements major enhancements to Dynamic Paint and Smoke Simulation that provide artistic users with enhanced operational flexibility in combination with better simulation performance levels. Artist efficiency grows because the updated simulation tools provide user-friendly brushes and realistic surface relations and precise density controls beyond achieving swift simulations that produce professional-quality effects. Blender 4.4 enables users to accomplish realistic fluid transitions and painting works alongside advanced smoke and fire creations through its powerful set of interactive tools.

CHAPTER SEVEN
WORKFLOW OPTIMIZATION
Add-ons & Scripting in Blender 4.4

Inside Blender's open-source environment the Add-ons and Scripting tools work as essential components because they let users develop Blender's features and design personalized workflow systems. The latest Blender 4.4 supports Python scripting alongside third-party add-ons which generates extensive functionality choices for artistic professionals together with software developers and technological team leaders. The section demonstrates recent capabilities and best practices of working with Add-ons and Scripting inside Blender 4.4.

1. Add-ons Updates in Blender 4.4

Add-ons within Blender have the ability to enhance software operation through their ability to provide fresh features with automatic workflow solutions as well as fresh user interface options. The latest Blender 4.4 version delivers multiple improvements for the add-on selection.

Add-ons Updates in Blender 4.4

A. Add-on Manager Improvements

In Blender 4.4 the Add-o Manager receives updates to optimize finding add-ons and handling installation procedures as well as add-on management.

1. **Faster Add-on Loading**: Fast Add-on Loading has become a feature of Blender 4.4 which enhances startup speed particularly during workflows using various add-ons. The ability to handle large numbers of add-ons in workflow becomes more efficient because of this enhancement.

2. **Search and Filter Enhancements**: Search and Filter Enhancements in The Add-on Manager deliver better add-on search results because users can now browse through categories alongside tags and functionality. The improved add-on search and

filter systems help users with numerous add-ons improve their workflow efficiency.

3. **Add-on Auto-Update**: Blender 4.4 offers an add-on auto-update functionality which enables automatically retrieving the newest version of installed extensions from Blender Market and external repositories. The feature keeps users on the current versions of their essential tools.

4. **Better Compatibility with Blender Versions**: Latest add-ons come with version control compatibility which detects the current Blender version and adjusts their features automatically. The constant detection between Blender version and add-on settings prevents problems when performing Blender updates and version switches.

B. New and Updated Add-ons

Blender 4.4 delivered new add-ons together with important updates to existing programs to enhance the users' experience.

1. **Asset Browser Integration**: Blender 4.4 created stronger connections between Asset Browser and add-ons by permitting users to browse and manage and store assets through the add-on interface. Users

can better manage their projects through easier asset reusability by storing materials models rigs and shades in multiple projects.

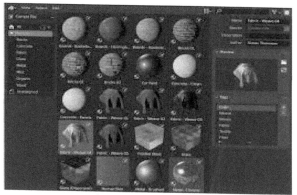

Asset Browser

2. **Expanded Simulation Add-ons**: Simulation-related add-ons in the latest release provide advanced simulation tools and updated functionality which results in improved visualization and accelerated simulation execution within the viewport.

3. **Modeling and Sculpting Add-ons**: The Blender 4.4 software release includes modeling and sculpting add-ons that enhance workflow functionality by delivering sophisticated brushes and improved topology tools and surface detailing

capabilities that merge into a single sculpting environment.

4. **Rendering and Lighting Add-ons**: These new add-ons improve rendering as well as lighting setups through preconfigured scenes and advanced HDRI libraries while offering simplified lighting setup control in Eevee as well as Cycles.

C. User Interface and Workflow Add-ons

Users can now customize their Blender 4.4 interface through enhanced tools that enhance their productivity across workflow operations:

1. **Workspace Customization Add-ons**: These allow for better workspace layouts, custom toolbars, and UI panels for specialized workflows. The new user interface allows artists to design personal interface settings which they can distribute to other artists.

2. **Task Automation Add-ons**: The new function of Task Automation Add-ons lets users create automated workflows for batch rendering and file organization and object selection and procedural model generation. Speedups throughout common operations result from these extra features which cut down manual labor duration.

2. Scripting in Blender 4.4

Python API in Blender functions as a robust feature through which users build scripts while creating personalized tools to automate various tasks. Blender 4.4 expands developer capabilities in scripting since it provides improved functionality for developers to insert custom features into Blender.

A. Python API Enhancements

1. **Simplified API for Add-on Development**: Blender 4.4 enables easier development of add-ons by simplifying its Application Programming Interface along with debugging and addition to add-on marketplaces. Blender 4.4 simplifies its API by offering more user-friendly methods that let developers interact with Blender core functionalities including mesh data alongside object management and scene layout tools which shortens add-on development and maintenance period.

2. **Enhanced Performance for Scripts**: The latest Blender 4.4 update has already improved script execution times across the Python scripting environment. The scripting functionality executes with increased performance while operating within multi-core CPUs and processing large datasets

related to complex simulations and persistent scene hierarchies.

3. **New Classes and Methods**: The Python API in Blender 4.4 introduces fresh classes and methods that enable work with advanced features including volumetric shaders and geometry nodes as well as viewport enhancement tools. Professional developers can retrieve and operate new capabilities through the latest version thanks to this interface.

B. Debugging and Development Tools

1. **Improved Scripting Editor**: The built-in Text Editor of Blender has gained enhanced capabilities through the addition of Python scripting syntax highlighing features together with improved automated code completion. Python scripting becomes more convenient through built-in features which enable writing testing and debugging without Blender interface disruption.

2. **Console Enhancements**: Blender 4.4 features an upgraded version of the Python Console that provides developers with better inspection tools for debugging purposes. A Python console allows you to perform interactive commands while expressions get live feedback on script changes in real-time

which makes debugging scripts and exploring new script ideas easier.

3. **Interactive Debugging**: The interactive debugger of Blender 4.4 enables users to establish breakpoints and perform step-by-step debugging of their code with runtime variable inspection features inside the scripting environment. Developers gain enhanced accuracy and control in their analysis of problems together with new functionality testing due to this feature.

C. Python Scripting for Animation & Rigging

1. **Animation Control**: The API functions in Blender 4.4 enable programmers to animate objects and meshes along with bones directly through Python programming scripts. Through Python developers find it simpler to generate animation procedures or construct unique rigging and controller systems.

2. **Rigging and Automation**: The Blender rigging system gained new Python capabilities which enable developers to produce advanced automated rigging systems with procedural character rigging capabilities. These tools provide users with expanded capabilities of customizing automated

workflows that include both character rigging systems and facial animation systems.

3. **Geometry Nodes via Python**: Python scripting enables users to interact completely with Geometry Nodes through scripts to create procedural models while animating them. The introduction of Python code editing for geometry node networks enables developers to achieve additional procedural control for artists.

3. New Scripting Features for Artists

Through new scripting features in Blender 4.4 users can develop their creative workflow using Python scripts without having to master programming concepts.

A. Customizable Tool Panels

The 4.4 version of Blender lets users develop their own custom tool panels together with UI elements via Python programming. Through the creation of interactive interfaces artists can modify fundamental project parameters by using easy buttons and sliders without accessing code or menus.

B. Python-Based Tool Creation

1. **Custom Tools and Operators**: Artists using Python scripts can develop both new tools along with operators that help them perform complex tasks more efficiently. By writing basic Python code an artist can automatically produce procedural patterns alongside creating basic mesh structures through interface buttons.

2. **UI Layouts for Artists**: Artists now can create their own customized UI layouts easier through an improved interface within Blender 4.4 which uses Python code as the foundation. Through Python programming artists can create their own customized toolbars and panels and menu elements that follow their individual projects and working methods.

C. Real-Time Customization

Blender 4.4 enables artists to get instant feedback regarding interface modifications as well as custom script additions through real-time interface updates. Users can test and adjust their scripts along with workflows in real time since restarting Blender or loading the script becomes unnecessary.

4. Conclusion

Python API development reaches new heights within Blender 4.4 because it provides both extensive scripting abilities and powerful development tools together with advanced add-ons availability. Through its performance enhancement and improved add-on integration along with its more intuitive scripting environment Blender 4.4 delivers the necessary developer and artist tools for customization and automation of workflow processes and custom tool development. Ruby Island Blender 4.4 builds an open creative platform tailored for both beginning automatizers working with elementary tasks and advanced programmers developing complex add-ons which enables 3D design and animation efficiency.

Performance Tips for Blender 4.4

The new Blender 4.4 release extends user-friendly performance boundaries to work optimally across multiple design projects including both simple models alongside complex animations and simulations. Efficient workflow optimization mechanics should be your priority when using the improved performance features of Blender. Multiple essential tips regarding speed optimization and time reduction together with workflow performance enhancement guide users through Blender 4.4 operations.

1. System Setup and Hardware Optimization

A. GPU vs. CPU Rendering

The Blender software includes GPU rendering capability supported by CUDA or OptiX for NVIDIA GPUs and OpenCL for AMD and CPU rendering functionality. The selection of system components according to hardware requirements proves critical for acquiring faster render times.

GPU vs. CPU Rendering

- **Use GPU Rendering for Faster Results**: Enabling GPU rendering from Render Properties panel results in faster outcomes when you use a system that includes CUDA or OptiX capable powerful GPUs. GPU devices outperform CPU units for rendering operations because they possess the ability to execute parallel operations.

- **Set the Appropriate Device**: Users of Blender 4.4 who have multiple GPUs can select which device to use for rendering. They also have the option to connect multiple GPUs for faster processing. Check your selected render device in Preferences > System > Cycles Render Devices.

- **Optimize CPU Rendering**: To optimize CPU rendering you must confirm your system meets the RAM requirements of heavy scenes. From the Preferences area access Threads to boost rendering performance by selecting how many threads should work during this process.

B. Memory Management

Rendering and performing advanced simulations require a great deal of memory taken up by RAM and video RAM. Blender 4.4 offers guidelines to better manage system memory use.

- **Increase Virtual Memory**: When your graphics card memory reaches capacity Blender will switch to swap space available on your hard drive. Increase your virtual memory until you meet requirements or upgrade your RAM..

- **Optimize Scene Complexity**: Load only the necessary high-quality textures and geometry objects to save memory space. Keep your modeling work piece as a proxy to let you do creative work before applying high-quality assets in the final render.

C. Optimize Preferences for Performance

Blender allows performance optimization through settings located in its Preferences section:

- **Enable Simplify**: You can lower scene complexity by switching on Render Properties Enable Simplify which reduces texture size and dims shadow quality while lowering sub-surface scattering detail. Using this setting makes the animation work easier on complex scenes.
- **Disable Auto-Save**: Activating auto-save uses too much system resources when applying it often to big scenes in Blender. You can modify your auto-save settings from Preferences > File including the option to turn it off.

- **Optimize Undo Settings**: Adjust automatic undo memory settings to work faster. The system performs better in editing large scenes when Blender stores fewer Undo actions in its memory.

2. Scene Optimization

A. Use Instances for Repeated Objects

Instances for objects that repeat throughout the scene will reduce memory load and boost execution speed.

Scene Optimization

- **Linked Duplicates (Instances)**: Duplicate linked objects with the Alt + D command instead of making new copies. Separate objects receive a single common mesh layout saving valuable memory space.
- **Use Collections for Instancing**: To handle large groups of instances effectively you should group

them into collections. You can optimize your scene better when you use this feature because it lets you modify many instances at once.

B. Use Layers and Viewport Visibility

The performance of complex scenes depends heavily on how you control what shows on the view screen. The viewport layers system lets you conceal task-specific elements that you don't need to view.

- **Use the "Viewport Display" Options**: In the Outliner change your view settings by turning off the visibility for objects you don't need to see at this time. To improve viewport movement efficiency hide secondary objects including complex simulations and background elements.

- **Disable Unnecessary Modifiers**: Turning off Subdivision Surface from your modifiers helps boost viewport performance. Turn off the Subdivision Surface modifier's sub-levels through the Modifiers panel until you need to edit them again. Activate the Apply function to set modifiers after completing your design work.

C. Use Low-Resolution Proxies for High-Detail Models

When working with intricate scenes reduce object complexity by creating simpler versions during the modeling, rigging and animation stages. Change low-resolution proxies from modeling to their high-resolution versions before rendering them.

- **Use Simplified Geometry**: Replace basic versions of assets with detailed geometry just before you render your work.

3. Viewport Optimization

A. Use Viewport Shading Appropriately

intense handling of visual effects pushes up system demand especially if shaders and textures have many details. To optimize performance:

- **Switch to Solid or Wireframe:** Turning Solid or Wireframe Viewport affects performance much less than material previews and rendered mode especially in complex scenes with textures and detailed geometry.
- **Disable Real-time Shadows**: Turning off real-time shadows during viewport navigation saves performance for computer systems. Using lightless

navigation will boost viewport speed when you need faster movement.

- **Limit the Number of Visible Objects**: Use collections in your viewport to make sure you see only a few selected objects. Use the Outliner to turn on and off visibility for items that you are not currently working on.

B. Reduce the Use of High-Resolution Textures

Using textures with high resolutions hurts performance speed. Here are some tips:

- **Use Lower Resolution Textures**: Adjust distance-dependent object textures to smaller resolutions when they are not in the camera's view. Apply high-resolution textures only to objects you focus on in close-ups.
- **Texture Compression**: Use PNG and JPEG texture types to save memory but monitor quality reduction during texture compression.

4. Rendering Optimization

A. Reduce Render Samples

Boosting sample count for clean renders in Cycles will create additional rendering time. Blender 4.4 includes several tools to render faster without losing image quality.

- **Denoising**: Blender 4.4 integrates an upgraded denoiser that smoothes out rendering artifacts to enable low sample counts at high quality. To speed up renders you can enable denoising in Eevee and Cycles which reduces image noise and lowers render times.
- **Adaptive Sampling**: scene complexity. Reducing render duration works best in straightforward parts to spare time but keeps higher test check in point by point zones.

B. Use Progressive Rendering with Eevee

Look for quick real-time performance by selecting Eevee as your Blender render motor since it offers fast comes about whereas creating high-quality pictures.

- **Use Simplified Lighting**: When rendering with Eevee you should turn off the advanced lighting options since they slow down performance. Make rendering faster by adjusting settings less detailed or lowering preview quality settings.

- **Optimize Reflections and Shadows**: When using Eevee customization tools adjust both shadow and reflection settings for quicker rendering while keeping good quality. When working with complex scenes you should lower the shadow resolution or restrict the areas covered by reflection probes to boost rendering speed.

5. Simulation Optimization

A simulation of fluid movement or smoke patterns demands substantial computer resources. Follow these recommendations to enhance output speed:

A. Use Simplified Simulations for Previews

For fast feedback during simulation work:

- **Lower Resolution**: Drop the simulation resolution in fluid smoke and cloth mode while working on previews. After achieving desired results raise the resolution for final simulations and rendering.
- **Bake Simulations**: When simulating fluids or smoke apply baking first to save processing power both during playback and final rendering.

B. Optimize Cache Settings

Complex simulation tasks complete faster when you control how memory settings work.

- **Use Disk Cache**: When processing bigger simulations you should store cache data to hard-disk instead of RAM to maintain performance levels.
- **Limit Cache Resolution**: Setting lower cache resolution specifically for fluid simulations makes simulation processing happen faster and faster. Adjust your simulation resolution upwards during the last quality check only.

6. Conclusion

Blender 4.4 contains multiple ways to make tasks run faster in all key areas such as rendering and simulations while handling scene elements better. You can enhance Blender's performance by updating your computer equipment while making Blender settings changes and decreasing scene details alongside appropriate rendering and simulation choices.

CHAPTER EIGHT

EXPORTING & FINAL OUTPUT

File Formats & Settings in Blender 4.4

In Blender 4.4 you can choose between various file types and settings to enable smooth transfers between programs and devices. When working with Blender 4.4 you need to understand both available file formats and proper settings to export content and save assets from different programs.

1. Supported File Formats in Blender 4.4

The version 4.4 update of Blender allows users to import and export files in many different formats including digital models, animations and texturing data. This section describes the major file formats that Blender 4.4 deals with:

A. 3D Model Formats

1. **.blend (Blender Project Files)**

   o **Description**: Blender's native file format. The Blender project features all project items such as models, textures, animations, materials, simulations, and render settings in one compact store.

   o **Usage**: The program lets you manage Blender file operations within its environment. Blender 4.4 enhances its ability to handle large project files and beads down the chances of file loss.

2. **.obj (Wavefront OBJ)**

   o **Description**: The .obj format becomes a reliable choice for users who export 3D geometry because it stores vertices, edges, and face information. Users can export and import simple mesh shapes and textured UV images from Blender 4.4.

   o **Usage**: You can use this format to transfer basic models across various 3D programs but the option for animation, rigging and multiple materials is not available.

3. **.fbx (Autodesk FBX)**

   o **Description**: FBX maximizes functionality by solving the delivery needs of detailed 3D objects with texture attachments and hierarchical setups as well as movements and light effects. Programmers widely apply .fbx files in computer graphics engines and 3D applications.

   o **Usage**: You can move created content into both Unreal Engine and Unity platform plus any other supported 3D tools. Blender 4.4 enhances how it handles the FBX format by improving data exchange both with rigged characters and their skin setups.

4. **.dae (Collada)**

   o **Description**: The XML-based open-standard provides a method for different 3D software applications to exchange assets. This file format includes all necessary data related to models and textures as well as animations together with scene parameters.

   o **Usage**: Usage of this format extends to multiple applications that include game engines and CAD software and 3D animation tools.

5. **.stl (Stereolithography)**

   o **Description**: The tool contains 3D printing format geometry information only which excludes texture and color specifications.

   o **Usage**: Through 3D printing or CNC machining the model requires export from Blender. Blender provides export capabilities through both ASCII and binary versions of STL format.

6. **.ply (Polygon File Format)**

   o **Description**: The format offers support for geometry features and includes properties regarding colors and normals. The 3D scanning process and point cloud data management both work with this file type.

   o **Usage**: The .ply format serves as a suitable choice when users need to export meshes obtained through scanning because it maintains extra characteristics such as color information.

7. **.3ds (3D Studio)**

   o **Description**: The 3D Studio format is an older data format which many applications still read. This file format saves 3D models and textures together with their materials although it lacks support for modern lighting techniques and animation capabilities.

   o **Usage**: Softerware vendors can transfer older models and assets through the legacy format because this platform still has active support.

B. Animation & Rigging Formats

1. **.abc (Alembic)**

   o **Description**: The .abc format enables application-to-application data transfer of complicated animation data formats. The format supports storage of geometrical data along with animation sequences and simulated elements such as hair and fluid movements.

   o **Usage**: This format serves animation laboratories particularly well when exchanging big animation sequences and simulation output as well as elaborate rig systems. This format delivers exceptional value when different departments within your production setting need to exchange data with their software systems.

2. **.bvh (Biovision Hierarchy)**

   o **Description**: A format named .bvh handles motion capture data transfer when working with rigs.

   o **Usage**: Import/export motion capture animation data for rigs or character animation work.

C. Texture & Image Formats

1. **.png (Portable Network Graphics)**
   - **Description**: The portable network graphics format serves users with lossless compression and transparency while being a popular selection. Users often employ .png because it excels in both image and texture applications for their 3D projects.
   - **Usage**: It is best to utilize .png files (with alpha channels) for creating transparent or lossless texture images.

2. **.jpg (JPEG)**
   - **Description**: The compressed image format .jpg provides optimal performance for photo and image files when file size matters.
   - **Usage**: Attract various background elements and big-scale map data by using this format because file size matters more than quality.

3. **.tiff (Tagged Image File Format)**
   - **Description**: The tiff image format provides high-quality performance through lossless compression which makes it an excellent option for professional rendering processes.

- Usage: These maps demand the .tiff (Tagged Image File Format) for their clariTy representation.

4. **.hdr (High Dynamic Range Image)**

   - **Description**: The HDR image format works as a specialized format to store environment textures through HDRI files and lighting information. The format offers broader color data storage for implementations that require realistic lighting.

   - **Usage**: For realistic lighting and reflection you should apply HDRI environment maps through this format.

5. **.exr (OpenEXR)**

   - **Description**: Professional rendering along with visual effects (VFX) work with .hdr files because they handle images that carry high dynamic range information.

   - **Usage**: The .exr file is optimal for film compositing because it handles complex light passes alongside other complex imaging data in post-production.

D. Other Formats

1. **.gltf / .glb (GL Transmission Format)**

   o **Description**: The modrn transmission standard enables users to exchange 3D models alongside animations as well as scenes. The format performs optimally during runtime operations because it serves web-based 3D applications.

   o **Usage**: Web applications and virtual reality as well as augmented reality projects may use these exported assets for their operations.

2. **.usd / .usdc (Universal Scene Description)**

   o **Description**: Carrying a framework developed by Pixar it functions as an exchange method for 3D assets particularly when applied to high-end production pipelines. Supports complex scene graphs, materials, animation, and simulation.

   o **Usage**: The creation and management of complicated VFX and animation pipelines occurs through use of .usd / .usdc files in high-end studios.

2. File Settings in Blender 4.4

Integration between files and external applications becomes more efficient through the optimized file settings available in Blender 4.4 that control storage management as well as import exporting functionality.

A. File Preferences

1. **Auto Save**

   o **Description**: The system implements an automatic backup feature which creates project reserves at fixed time points.

   o **Settings**: Users can modify both file auto-save duration and the number of saved files under Preferences > File.

   o **Tip**: The auto-save frequency should be set higher when you work on large projects because this strategy prevents your work from being lost if Blender crashes.

2. **Temporary File Directory**
   - ○ **Description**: The temporary data files that Blender saves like auto saves and cache files and render outputs are directed to the pathway specified in this setting.
   - ○ **Settings**: Through the settings you can specify an alternative storage location to separate project files from your main folder structure so your temporary files end up in a disk space adequate for handling them.
3. **File Compression**
   - ○ **Description**: The option enables compression of .blend files which results in decreasing file sizes.
   - ○ **Settings**: In the File menu under Save Preferences you can find the compression features of Blender. The file compression feature becomes beneficial for maintaining large file sizes or internet file transfers.

B. Import/Export Settings
   1. **FBX Export Settings**
      - ○ **Description**: Blender users can modify FBX export parameters through this setting to

handle mesh and animation and material content export processes.

o **Settings**: The export process allows users to select between armatures and meshes and animation keyframe transmission. The latest Blender 4.4 version provides enhanced support for FBX export by establishing better compatibility with shape keys together with rigging systems and UV map functionality.

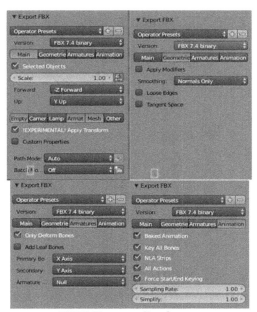

FBX Export Settings

213

2. **GLTF Export Settings**

   o **Description**: You can determine how geometry together with materials and animations export when using the .gltf or .glb format.

   o **Settings**: Settings enable users to include animations while they embed textures for configuring material settings that optimize model exportation when targeting web and game environments.

3. **OBJ Export Settings**

   o **Description**: The OBJ export process allows users to configure mesh and material features as well as texture handling parameters for the .obj data format.

   o **Settings**: The export options let users choose which object groups together with materials and UV maps will be exported. The .obj file format does not include either animation sequences or rig data during the export process.

4. **Alembic Export Settings**

   o **Description**: The program Alembic functions as a tool for exporting animated meshes together with scene data.

   o **Settings**: Blender 4.4 enables users to determine the export of geometry alone or animation motion or both simultaneously. The level of motion data precision you want to export is something you can directly control while preparing complex simulation or rig exports.

Alembic Export Settings

3. Best Practices for Managing Files in Blender

- **Organize Your Assets**: Access and manage your assets easier through organization using Blender's Asset Browser management feature. Large design projects benefit from this feature because it enables management of multiple textures together with models and animations.

- **Use External References**: The preferred approach to handling large projects includes using Linked Files instead of appending assets because this method helps preserve file size and avoid file bloat issues. Working with external libraries and collaborating with others becomes more efficient through the use of this function.

- **Version Control**: The implementation of version control systems becomes essential for Blender files during team projects because it ensures proper maintenance and file tracking. Version control systems like Git will track changes in your project files through the implementation of a tool.

4. Conclusion

Users can make Blender 4.4 suitable for multiple workflows through its broad range of supported file systems including 3D models and animations and textures and simulations. Enhancing your workflow occurs when you learn to optimize file import/export techniques and settings because this facilitates easy asset sharing between different platforms and applications. Mastering these file formats together with Blender's settings enables full-scale utilization of the program in small and big projects.

Rendering for Different Platforms in Blender 4.4

Rendering features of Blender 4.4 deliver exceptional performance for multiple platforms such as desktop computers and cloud-based environments as well as game engine uses. Proper configuration of Blender rendering settings across different platforms creates conditions that deliver peak quality output along with top performance and works smoothly with every platform. The section demonstrates how to configure rendering setups along with CPU/GPU computing and cloud-based computation systems and game engine connectivity.

1. CPU vs. GPU Rendering

Both CPU rendering and GPU rendering are the main rendering options that Blender 4.4 delivers to users. Your decision of which platform to use depends on the type of platform which leads to better performance.

CPU vs. GPU Rendering

A. CPU Rendering

- **Description**: The system processor serves as the basis for CPU rendering to generate the render results. The process of CPU rendering achieves more stability in particular situations yet it completes tasks at a slower speed in comparison to GPU rendering for all visuals except heavy and memory-intense scenes.

- **Platform Use**: Best for systems with powerful CPUs but less powerful GPUs. The process works well when GPU resources are minimal in a system context.

- **Settings**:
  - o Users should choose CPU rendering from the Render Properties > Device options within Cycles.
  - o **Advantages**: The main advantage of CPU-based rendering is its greater flexibility since CPUs typically have larger available RAM capacities in comparison to GPU memory resources.
  - o **Disadvantages**: The main drawback of using CPU rendering is that it renders slower than GPU rendering options.

B. GPU Rendering

- **Description**: The GPU render process executes computations through your system graphics card. GPU technology was built for parallel computing tasks and this leads to rapid rendering performance apart from producing optimal results for complex graphics with lighting and shading features.
- **Platform Use**: Best for platforms with powerful GPUs, such as workstations, laptops with dedicated graphics cards, or high-performance servers.

- **Settings**:
    - ○ Users must choose the render device in Cycles under Render Properties > Device through CUDA (NVIDIA devices) or OptiX (RTX NVIDIA devices) or OpenCL (AMD devices).
    - ○ **Advantages**: Quick rendering times are achievable with the selected settings specifically for sophisticated scenes that have detailed elements. The data processing speed of lighting effects along with shaders and textures becomes much higher for GPUs when compared to CPUs.
    - ○ **Disadvantages**: The GPU depends on its own VRAM storage to render scenes but when working with large scenes the GPU might not have sufficient memory capacity for powerful GPUs.

C. Hybrid Rendering (CPU + GPU)

- **Description**: The computer program Blender enables synchronous operation between CPU and GPU capabilities for rendering purposes. The blended rendering arrangement employments CPU and GPU capabilities to quicken the method whereas taking advantage of their best highlights.

- **Platform Use**: Useful for high-end workstations with both powerful CPUs and GPUs. Virtual memory allocation through rendering aids users whose artwork exceeds the standard GPU memory capacity of one device.
- **Settings**:
  - Under the Render Properties > Device section of Cycles users should activate CPU and GPU.
  - **Advantages**: Decision to utilize all available system resources leads to faster completion times because of maximum performance output.
  - **Disadvantages**: The optimal performance requires specific configuration adjustments in certain rendering platforms.

2. Cloud Rendering

Cloud services enable users to distribute their rendering processes to remote servers through their cloud infrastructure. Users without top-end devices or those managing large-scale projects can benefit from this particular feature because it consumes their limited computing power properly.

A. Using Blender's Own Cloud Render

The Blender 4.4 update includes Blender Cloud integration which enables users to connect with subscription-based render farm resources known as high-powered farm solutions. The Blender ecosystem integrates this service seamlessly while providing professional tools for collaboration and asset management to users.

- **Platform Use**: Studio users who lack expensive hardware systems can optimize their workflow through the Platform Use feature.
- **Settings**: Users can establish Blender Cloud connection through the Cloud tab located in the Render Properties section. The system enables faster results after you set up your project and upload it to the cloud rendering service.
- **Advantages**: The system allows users to adjust computational power use on demand and billing only reflects actual used resources.
- **Disadvantages**: Costs related to cloud-use as well as time needed for larger scene uploads or

downloads represent the main disadvantages of this service.

B. Third-Party Cloud Rendering Services

Users of Blender can access scalable render farms through the third-party cloud services including RebusFarm, Render Street and Sheep It Render Farm. Cloud services perform the rendering of your Blender file and assets by accepting uploaded content which they convert to rendered frames.

- **Platform Use**: Users who work in professional studios or as freelancers with deadline pressures should consider this platform because it provides the power needed for handling complex scenes along with complex animations.
- **Settings**: To use the platform you must upload your project files followed by configuring the rendering parameters like resolution and samples while working with the individual upload tool of the service.
- **Advantages**: Fast and scalable rendering power with minimal setup. In addition to flexibility you can perform work from any location without buying costly hardware systems.

- **Disadvantages**: The cost of this service grows rapidly when rendering large or sophisticated renders. Server accessibility and network velocity determine the length of time it takes for the process to complete.

3. Rendering for Game Engines

Blender users need to make crucial adjustments to both file formats and settings when exporting assets for Unity and Unreal Engine integration to reach design targets about performance and compatibility.

A. Exporting for Unity and Unreal Engine

The game engines Unity and Unreal Engine accept numerous importing formats which include models and animations with textures and materials. FBX glTF and OBJ stand among the predominant file formats during Blender-to-game engine conversion processes.

1. **FBX Export**:
   - **Platform Use**: It serves many industries for the export of animated assets with models and rigs. This format suits models and characters of high complexity which need skeletal movements.

- Settings:
  - Under **File > Export**, select **FBX**.
  - The export settings should fit the requirements by enabling animations and transform baking and applying unit measurements for Blender scale conversion to the game engine units.
- **Advantages**: The FBX exporter enables wide support from Unity and Unreal Engine for animation responses and mesh transport and material adoption.
- **Disadvantages**: The restrictions of FBX occur when dealing with intricate systems and difficulties emerging from differences between Blender and the game engine values.

-

225

2. **glTF Export**:

   ○ **Platform Use**: Web-based 3D apps along with game engines and real-time applications use glTF as their preferred modern efficient format to represent 3D scenes and models.

   ○ **Settings**:

   ▪ Under File > Export, select glTF (.glb).

   ▪ The export process should include options for animations in addition to materials and textures. The performance-optimized .glb binary file holds all modeling resources (textures and animations) in one container.

   ○ **Advantages**: The lightweight nature of glTF as well as its real-time rendering optimized format makes it suitable for performance-critical applications.

   ○ **Disadvantages**: The FBX exporter does not support complex features at the same level as other complex rigging or shader processes require FBX.

3. **OBJ Export**:

   o **Platform Use**: Platform Use offers a basic format to store static meshes together with textures while ignoring animation or rigging information.

   o **Settings**:

     ▪ Under File > Export, select OBJ.

     ▪ You should enable all essential features regarding texture paths and UV mapping when exporting.

   o **Advantages**: Static models with minimal rigging requirements find optimal solutions through OBJ export due to its basic nature.

   o **Disadvantages**: Rigging as well as complex materials and animations are not supported when using the OBJ Export process.

B. Optimizing Assets for Game Engines

Game engine performance will reach its optimal levels after Blender users optimize all exported assets by addressing geometry complexity together with material properties and texture demand.

- **Reduce Polygon Count**: The Decimate Modifier or manual mesh simplification methods should be used

227

to minimize polygon counts in order to enable real-time rendering.

- **Bake Textures**: The transportation of texture data as baked data like normals, lighting and shadows results in fewer computational requirements for the game engine in real time.

- **Use Efficient Textures**: Efficient texturing requires compression along with resolution selection based on real-time rendering demands. The implementation of PBR workflows for realistic material handling represents a best practice within game engines to produce realistic results.

4. Multi-Platform Rendering

Blender 4.4 enables setup of rendering across diverse platforms which incorporates desktops and cloud services along with game engines. These guidelines will help you achieve efficient multi-platform rendering setup:

- **Distributed Rendering**: Teams with extensive members can achieve distributed rendering by dividing their tasks between multiple machines. Two rendering tools help achieve this task: Blender's Network Render along with third-party services.

- **Cross-Platform Consistency**: The renderings must display uniformity between every operational system. The glTF and Alembic file formats safeguard your scene properties including animation and materials when moving between different platforms.
- **Render Previews**: A low-resolution preview rendering function on lesser powerful machines saves time before running high-quality renders on more advanced systems for cross-platform projects.

5. Conclusion

The rendering environment in Blender 4.4 permits flexibility to match a range of platforms which include computers and cloud farms and gaming systems. Proficiency in platform-specific settings for CPU, GPU, cloud rendering and game engines will help users produce quick efficient high-quality renders. Blender 4.4 features all required tools needed for diverse rendering needs to enable studio work in both film production and game development alongside architectural visualization.

www.ingramcontent.com/pod-product-compliance
Lightning Source LLC
LaVergne TN
LVHW051323050326
832903LV00031B/3326